And That Day Came

"Acceptance"

Jacqulyn E. Grant

BALBOA.
PRESS
A DIVISION OF HAY HOUSE

Balboa Press books may be ordered through booksellers or by contacting:

Balboa Press
A Division of Hay House
1663 Liberty Drive
Bloomington, IN 47403
www.balboapress.com
1 (877) 407-4847

Print information available on the last page.

ISBN: 978-1-9822-0972-8 (sc)
ISBN: 978-1-9822-0974-2 (hc)
ISBN: 978-1-9822-0973-5 (e)

Library of Congress Control Number: 2018909130

Balboa Press rev. date: 08/21/2018

To my wonderful son, Brooks

To my late parents, Fannie Estelle and Benjamin Sr.

To my late grandparents, Floyd and Pearl

To each one of my sisters, Lyndia (ex-husband Ronald), Ernestine, and La-Forest ("Franquis")

To all my brothers, Freddie (wife Carolyn), Benjamin Jr. (wife Carolyn), Elton Leon [deceased] (wife Ruth), Dalton (wife Gayle), Shelton, and Felton

To one of my several beautiful nieces, Tanika (husband Arioty), and her absolutely lovely daughter, Lola, both spiritually enlightened who bring me peace and great joy

To my best friend, Jacqueline, for always being there, listening, and providing her unwavering love and support over many precious decades

To all my beautiful nieces and handsome nephews, Kitty, Bob and Missy, Terri and Kelley, Ease and Yogi, Dalton Jr., Michael, David, Colleen, Matthew, Tausha, and Aijon

To all my grand and great-nieces and nephews; all my loving and supportive aunts in North Carolina, Baltimore, and New York; my handsome uncles in North Carolina; and my close friends in Washington, DC, and Maryland who have kept in touch with me throughout the years

To my very special intuitive studies instructor, Terri Tucker, and all the members of my tribe who attended the January 2017 Intuitive Studies class in Phoenix, Arizona

To Jo Amidon for Star Family knowledge

To Heather Harder for my spiritually inspired trip to Cairo, Egypt, and Petra, Jordan

I've learned many valuable lessons from each of you. Thank you.

Contents

Introduction

M y angels gave me the title of this book more than thirty years ago. No, I didn't know a thing about help from angels back then, but I have no doubt today that they were with me all the time. I just didn't know.

One bright, sunny spring morning, the title of this book popped into my mind. The angel words were so powerful until I jumped out of bed and wrote down the title, *And That Day Came*. I tucked it away safely, and it never left my mind. I didn't act on it right then, but I knew deep inside that I would write a book with this title someday. It was back in the early 1990s, a time when my mind couldn't have been farther away from spirituality and the amazing wonders that exists.

When I look back on all the hints and symbols sent my way, I no longer feel badly that I paid no attention. Truth is, I simply could not pay attention and focus on what I didn't know existed. I couldn't imagine my life or myself in a deeper or more spiritual way because I simply wasn't ready to see, hear, or know that anything or anyone else existed as it relates to the spirit world.

As a young single mom trying to create a comfortable life for my son, I was caught up in my very busy life. We lived in a nice apartment in the suburbs, and I had a very demanding job in the city working for a politician. I asked one of my sisters to live with me because I needed help with my son, especially in the evenings while I finished undergraduate studies on weekends, followed by graduate studies in the evenings. She moved in, and what a relief! It was great seeing the two of them, nephew and aunt, bonding.

I received my bachelor of arts degree in May 1996, and I took the summer off. That fall, I began graduate school. I was certainly challenged by working full time in a political environment, while taking classes at night, but not every night.

Luckily I didn't have to worry about my young teenage son. When the dust settled, I realized that I needed more money for my budget. So I found another job out of the political arena, and it paid a bit more in higher education. Months later, in 1998, I earned my master of arts degree and decided not to attend my commencement. I joined my family, and we all packed up and drove down to my nephew's graduation to receive his bachelor of science degree from Morehouse College in Atlanta, Georgia. He's my oldest sister's oldest son. I chose to be with family on his graduation day, the same date as mine, which turned out to be a great decision. Yes, those were the good ol' days.

When I returned to work, fully armed with my new graduate degree, I was so excited and no doubt assured that things would finally change for the best. I waited to be called into my boss's office, as others did, to discuss a raise, promotion, or a new position that included more responsibility and money. Nothing happened.

I looked around and noticed that others who earned degrees were moving right along and getting ahead after they earned degrees. That's what I thought I was in line for too. I got nothing and felt like Charlie Brown. "I got a rock."[1]

I thought, *Oh, that's how it goes. You have to be in a clique to move up.*

That didn't set well with me at all. Plus, I learned many lessons from a boss who was tough and a perfectionist, but she also had lots of admirable character, strength, and courage. Nonetheless I immediately began to look for another position within that same institution.

I would move around every two to three years or so. That was how I moved up and gave myself promotions while staying with the same employer for more than eighteen years. Yes, I moved around a lot because I have a naturally curious brain with a knack for adapting to different situations. I get bored easily doing the same type of work year after year. My hat's off to all who choose to stay in one position over many years because, Lord knows, that's not for me. I really love learning and doing new things.

During the latter part of my self-directed promotions, I began to feel different somehow. It was as though something changed or shifted inside my soul. It was right after 9-11. Life for me was never the same. I began searching and searching for

---

[1] *It's the Great Pumpkin, Charlie Brown*, 1966.

the right position, but even after changing jobs several times, my heart just wasn't in the work. I'd sit there some days and ask, "Why am I here? There has to be more to life than this."

I knew that life had much more to offer, and I needed to fill that void and know that my work was meaningful and helped others. Instead I was clueless about beginning a search for a more meaningful job and life in general because more was as illusive as trying to stop a breeze from flowing through my fingers.

Today I know that *more* dwells inside of me. More was there all the time—my spirit, higher self, and many intuitive abilities along with all the wonderful archangels. I finally woke up and tapped in.

If we pay close attention, we would see the many messages, signs, or hints that our angels sent to us. For example, if you wake up at the same exact time for several consecutive nights or early mornings or if you see the same numbers on buildings, doors in movies, and television, you should know that these are all signs or hints from your angels.

Some of us are given hints through repeating words that we suddenly hear on television, radio, and the mouths of others. Other people receive pennies, nickels, dimes, and so on in odd places. I tend to find feathers.

Recently while living in Arizona, I had concerns at work, and one day, I walked into my office and found a feather on the floor right beside my chair. I picked it up with a smile and thought, *I have such loving angels with me all the time.*

Hints are also sent to us through symbols in nature, like a private rainbow in your own front yard or backyard or shapes of fluffy clouds that appear to resemble something or someone near and dear to your heart. Sometimes we are given our most meaningful hints through repeating dreams.

Why do these repeating numbers, patterns, symbols, and dreams happen? Is it coincidence? No. There are no coincidences. Everything—and I mean everything—happens in divine order.

We are all sent messages from our angels because they are trying to get our attention to wake up! Yes, our angels want us to wake up and really experience life to the fullest and at our best. We gain more out of life by going deep inside where love, peace, joy, and happiness dwells in abundance, which is through meditation. There, we learn about our experiences and ourselves, and we have a chance to really understand our past, which helps us to march on into the future.

There in this very sacred place, we see the wonders of the truly eye-opening reality of who we are as it comes to us and as it's received. For me, I find it amazing to go there, communicate, and return with an answer or better understanding of a concern or situation I'm currently facing. Yes, meditation is key for more overall self-awareness. Meditation is there for all of us to connect through spiritual awakening and to receive a glimpse in the spirit world to help us understand all that was planned for us during this incarnation.

We all experience good times and sometimes the opposite. We strive to learn those heartfelt lessons in life and move on while continuing to grow. Sometimes the unexpected catches us way off guard, which, if allowed, can and will linger on in our lives indefinitely. Life-changing moments tend to take our breath away and remain deep in our hearts and subconscious for many years and, for some, over many lifetimes. Some of us are destined to relive what we think are terrible moments over and over again, which in turn becomes our private hell because of the guilt piled on day by day.

We are creators. We make and shape our own lives. If we're not careful and face whatever challenge placed before us, our bodies will absorb every ugly drop of misery that in turn swells into disease or *dis-ease* that our doctors confirm. When that happens, most of us will then find the time to pray. *Dis-ease* causes us to realize that both life and time left to spend with loved ones is very precious.

Today is really all that we have. Why does it take something like *dis-ease* or near-death experiences to cause us to finally see, feel, and know that we should have spent more time with family and dear friends? But more importantly, those life-changing moments show us that we could have spent more time doing something each day that brings us joy. Yes, we all need to participate in something that brings us joy as often as possible. But that's the thing: there are no mistakes, only lessons. If we had known to do something differently at a given time, we would have. We all do the best we can with what we have at every precise moment in time.

I've lived through many personal storms and held on to life with determination and a weather-beaten heart. It's difficult to find safe footing after any private devastation. Sometimes I've wondered and asked God, "Why me? What did I do to ever deserve this?"

Many days and nights, I thought God forgot I existed, or I simply felt invisible. In hindsight, I realize now that He was there with me all the time. It's hard to imagine going through such deep, mental anguish with Him by my side, especially such deep pain and anguish. Some days, the pain was unbearable, so I'd just take a nap in the day or have a nightcap and go to bed early just to shut off my brain and to stop thinking about my problems. I held my own pity parties, starring me!

Luckily I knew when to end that show of tears. As I awake to a new day, the problem is still there, but it's never as taxing or grueling as before. Why does everything feel, look, and seem so differently after a good night's sleep? I've often pondered these questions in the past. But when you're going through a crisis, after you pray and have a good night's sleep, you'll notice the brilliant sunshine and the sound of birds chirping. You'll hear the wind blow through leaves and tree limbs. All help lighten the load of concerns and burdens from just the day and night before.

Sometimes we know deep in our heart that we should do something else, something different and meaningful with our lives. That's our inner voice, trying to guide us in the direction of our life's path. But we choose to ignore those feelings and continue on with the status quo. Why? Because it's easy. Easy then becomes a not so good habit. It's very easy to ignore hunches and gut feelings about ourselves, especially when our thoughts are not aligned with our instincts.

Timing is everything. If we have low self-esteem for whatever reason, the right time to make a change will never come along because of the dwelling in the never-ending loop of lower frequencies. If we don't stop that cycle, pay attention, and really see what's going on in our lives, we may never make those plans to move forward and make a true difference in our lives. So, yes, it really is easy to continue on with what we know, even though every cell in our body tells us otherwise. I learned that lesson the hard way ... *twice.*

Ever since my early teens, I knew that I never, ever wanted to work in an office. At that young age, I knew then that I loved the arts. I loved to travel and wanted to see the world. I never wanted to be cooped up in a stuffy ol' office all day, attending meetings, and doing work that I could care less about.

Ironically, 90 percent or more of my work life has been just that, cooped up in a stuffy ol' office doing what I really could care less about. I chose what I didn't want because it felt like the right thing to do. It felt safe.

It sounds like I'm talking about a boring man or marriage! But for me, a safe office job is or equals boring. If I already knew how I felt about my wants in life so long ago, why did I make such a hard bed for myself?

It's simple. I had not yet discovered my life's passion. I didn't know myself or how important I really was in the eyes of God. That lack of knowledge created an uphill path to what I did not want. I was going nowhere fast and manifesting more and more of what I didn't want because that was my focus. Plenty of single women out there do what they love. On one hand, I wanted to be a singer, actor, or dancer or to have a career of some kind in the arts.

On the other hand, I did nothing toward attaining a career in the arts. Instead I caged myself in an office, aged, and watched the world go by while trying to make the best of my life. The only joy was knowing that I could provide for my son because now I was a very responsible parent. Like so many others, I went back and forth to work every day, just as if we were herds of cattle. I wanted him to be happy and to enjoy life because his happiness meant a lot to me. My own happiness didn't make the list.

As time went by, I developed—and still manage—high blood pressure, and I contend with hypothyroidism. I wasn't living my best life because I disregarded all that inspired me. I've learned that, if I were really passionate about working in the arts, I would have done something about it decades ago. I realize now that I was not even torn. How's that for a fact?

My passion was being a responsible parent. In my eyes, that meant I needed to sacrifice all of my hopes and dreams to provide a stable life for my son. On top of that, I carried the guilt and burden of not being married, and my son's dad was never a part of his life. It was inevitable that my son became first in my life and to a fault, I might add. As for me, I unwittingly gave up everything and forgot about myself in the process. What was my life really like? To sum it all up in one word, it was empty.

One day, I began to think about all the things that I allowed to happen and suddenly realized that I'd forgotten about my happiness and myself in the process. I finally understood that it was my choice to stay in bondage at work and continue the daily grind with an unrewarding and unfulfilling job. It was up to me to make a change. My life has always been in my hands because I was the creator who ran that show.

Now I'm following my newfound passion in the arts as a writer. Oh yeah, I love to write! I've learned that things really do work out for the best when you follow your gut instincts and have passion for what you do. It's extra special if what brings you joy also helps others along the way.

I realize now that everything experienced in my life helped me to become the person I am today. Remember, there are no accidents, only lessons, and everything happens as it should as you exercise a right to free will. Each experience, sometimes repeated, is a lesson in life. I'm stronger and more focused today because of those lessons. Now I listen to my body music, or gut instinct, and see the many signs sent from my angels.

When I was about age thirteen, I noticed the number 640. It was part of a license plate belonging to one of my sister's boyfriends. For some reason, I made up a silly statement and would say it in a very goofy voice to memorize the entire license plate. I couldn't forget that license plate if I tried. I committed the plate to memory just in case something happened to her and if someone needed to give that information to the police. For some odd reason, I didn't trust him. So memorizing that license plate as a goofy statement worked.

To this very day, that same number catches my attention. Back then, I wondered why I continued to notice that number and dismiss it from my thoughts. Years later, and as I've become more curious about astrology and numerology, I decided to add the three digits together to find out what it meant. So here we go:

$$640 \text{ equals } 6 + 4 + 0 = 10$$
$$\text{The sum of } 10 \text{ equals } 1 + 0 = 1$$

The number one relates to pioneering, new beginnings, creation, independence, and so on. Although I was very young, about age thirteen, when the number 640 first appeared in my life, I wasn't ready for any of this stuff and didn't know anything about spiritual connections, metaphysics, or spirituality.

Decades later, the next number the angels sent my way was 781. Well, we know:

$$7 + 8 + 1 = 16$$
$$1 + 6 = 7$$

The number seven is my life path number. I'll share a little more later in the first chapter about the significance of my life path number, seven, sent to me from the angels.

It means a lot to know that I have loving support for this book from my son, Brooks; all my sisters, Lyndia, Ernestine, and Franquis; my best friend, Jacqueline; my niece, Tanika, and her daughter, Lola; and finally Terri Tucker and Heather Harder.

I'm now ready to take a chance on me. Yahoo! All of the many instances shared with you thus far have had great meaning in my life, and hopefully you will find at least one story or instance that resonates with you. Life has a whole lot to offer, and I'm ready for the journey. Yes, I know I have a lot to learn, and while carving out my new life, I'll absorb all I can while I can because it's such a great feeling to know that I'm okay. Change is good!

Oh, by the way, can you say *Abraham*? (Esther Hicks, inspirational speaker and author, teaches audiences through "a collective consciousness from a nonphysical dimension" called Abraham.) Some of you get my point, while others will get it when they are ready to be ready to be ready!

It is my intention to help others realize their natural gifts and to become more aware about gut feelings and intuition. Remember to love yourself and treat yourself well. Always trust your gut instincts by paying close attention to your feelings about others and yourself. Be sure to observe your environment as it relates to Mother Earth. You will soon begin to notice messages from your angels. Know that you are watched over from above and loved by many: your ancestors, angels, and God.

Namaste.

Part I

God really doesn't give us more than we can bear. There comes a time in each of our lives when we must stop, recognize, and decide to either continue our current path or simply choose another that feels right.

Chapter 1

Aloof

Be True to Yourself

Like a hurricane swirling deeply through troubled water, my life was out of control. I didn't know what to do or where to turn. The angels knew I was ready for this hard lesson, but I ignored every sign along the way. They helped by pushing me out of a dead-end job. If only I'd opened my eyes sooner and paid attention to moments like those before, I would have actually seen the cluttered path that I created for myself, time and time again. That was my world—paths of destruction with many hurricane seasons.

Now it's time to rebuild. I realize that all my life's work, good or questionable, led me to this very moment. When I stop and think about everything, I realize that I felt isolated and alone as a child, and those feelings tend to creep up as an adult to this very day. But before I could be true to myself, I had to remember how I came to be.

1

I was born Monday, December 7, at exactly eleven o'clock at night. I am the seventh child of nine—yes, by the same two married parents—and the number seven is no doubt my lucky, or life path number. My mother said I was born with a veil over my face. She knew I was born with intuitive gifts like her. I call my older siblings, or the first five children that Mother had, the "first family" because she actually planned to stop having children after the fifth child was born.

The first family includes my two older brothers and three sisters. All were born and raised down south and attended school there. Mom spent a lot of time with them. She had meals prepared when they came home from school, but more importantly, she was home a lot at the end of their school day.

Life was very different back then because my parents were younger and more vibrant and had more energy to manage farm work while bringing up disciplined and well-mannered children. It was tough on my dad being a sharecropper. And it was hard on my oldest brother, who worked a lot with Dad and missed many days from high school due to farming. When we were adults, my brother told me that he looked forward to rainy days or bad weather so he could go to school. There was no farming in the rain.

I have a sketchy memory of my little life in North Carolina, but I do recall one Sunday as we were all getting ready for church. I couldn't have been more than two or three, and I was wearing a little pink dress that day. Before going to church, my oldest brother shined my black patent leather shoes with one of Mom's homemade biscuits. I watched him break the bread in half. He used half the biscuit on each shoe. Then he wiped my shoes until both shined.

And boy oh boy, my little mind was wondering about what I saw, trying to connect food to shoes, but my shoes were shiny! I was so happy too. He picked me up, and we all left for church. That's the only time I remember any of my brothers doing something or anything for me while we lived in North Carolina.

I came along in the "second family," consisting of the last four, all unplanned children. I know that's a lot of unplanned children, but we were dearly loved just the same. The second family includes my older brother, myself, and two younger brothers. Life for us was very different. We were raised in the big fast city up north instead of the peacefully slow South. Mom and Dad worked hard on their jobs in the city, and most days, there was no one home to greet us after school. And there were definitely no hot meals. But our family pet anxiously waited for someone—anyone—to come home. He was a beautiful, black Newfoundland with a great big heart.

At the time, I was about five years old and afraid of him. He loved to play. He'd scratch me with his paws, and it really hurt. I was afraid he'd scratch me, so every day after school, I felt terrorized by our dog. He would jump up to me, and I thought the world was coming to an end. I thought I was being attacked.

Years later, I realize that he was only playing with me. Sometimes my sister-in-law, who was married to my oldest brother, was there when I came home from school. In fact, she took me on my first day of school. I'll never forget that day because I was really nervous.

No one else could ever take the place of my mom. I think I was in love with her. I couldn't wait for her to get home from work. I would watch the clock and walk two blocks to greet her at the bus stop every day. Oh, how my heart would fill with love and joy when I saw her step off that big city bus. She always greeted me with a big smile, and she'd allow me carry her purse. This became our ritual.

Sometimes while playing with my friends, I'd miss her stepping off the bus and would see her walking up the street. I'd stop doing everything and make a mad dash down the street to greet her. I had to see her beautiful face with her guaranteed smile. That was my time alone with her, and I cherished every moment. On evenings and weekends, I was like her shadow. I followed her around the house everywhere.

My mother was the cleanest women I have ever known. She could make anything beautiful after cleaning it and giving a room or an entire house a little love. Guests would always comment about how everything was always so neat and clean. My mom could sew too. She made curtains, some of our clothes, and many other things. She taught me how to crochet doilies and afghans, and she taught me how to cornrow hair.

But she had her rules too. I did my chores and hung out with her a lot in the kitchen while she prepared meals. My mother was the best cook on the planet. She could cook anything! She had no specialty because she cooked everything and everything was super delicious. I'd sit at the table while she peeled peaches or apples when she made cobblers. She would peel the apples or peaches, and my little hands were held out, catching those

4

peelings and eating them as fast as I could. When she baked cakes, I'd wait for the mixing bowl and the big spoon. Um, good!

She told me once, "Baking is very sensitive. You have to be in the right mood and add love for baked goods to come out right." As an adult, I've done that every time.

Holidays were the best. For Thanksgiving, our home was filled with so much love, banana pudding, an assortment of cakes, sweet potato pies, apples and oranges, pecans, walnuts, Brazil nuts and peanuts, turkey and stuffing, fried chicken, ham, pot roast, collard greens, string beans, cabbage, potato salad, mashed potatoes, corn, baked beans, black-eyed peas, lima beans, hush puppies, cornbread, and homemade biscuits. Yes, holidays were special. All the grown-up women would help, but my mother ran the show. We would eat together and enjoy ourselves with great food that would last several days after the holiday.

For Christmas, toys were scarce, but we certainly ate well. My parents did the very best they could for us with what they had. That means they guided us along with the knowledge they had, and they helped financially when they could to meet our needs. Most of the time, we, the second family, didn't get anything for Christmas, but the holiday feast was always a great joy because the whole family would be together, having a good ol' time.

I recall hearing that the boys and girls in the first family did get toys and the boys would pull off the doll heads and play baseball with them. Oh yeah, in the first family my brothers were the oldest and in charge of the girls. You know how that goes. The two older boys were over the three younger girls. They survived.

5

One year, I don't recall how my immediate older brother got a new bicycle, an English Racer. I wanted to ride that bike really bad. He was the oldest in the second family, and I was next in line with two younger brothers. Anyway, it was a boy's bicycle, and it was hard to figure out how to get situated on the thing to ride it.

One day, he said, "Don't touch my bike. I'll know if you did."

I thought, *Okay, just wait until you're not around. I'm gonna be on that bike before you can blink.*

And that day came when I had my way on that big bike for boys. I was about six years old and very willful. I took that bike out into the alley behind our row house. We lived at the top of the hill, and at the end of the alley stood a tall, brick wall of an apartment building. To the right of the building was a busy main street with lots of traffic, and to the left was a neighborhood street with some traffic. I angled myself up onto the bike and started riding down the alley. I didn't know that the little hill would cause the bike to go faster than I could control. I tried to use the brakes on the handlebars, but my little hands were too small for a good grip.

I thought, *Which way will I turn?*

I knew all about the traffic to my right and to my left. So I decided to keep straight and crashed into that brick wall of the apartment building. I was hoping the bike would hit the wall and bounce off safely. That didn't happen. I don't remember hitting the wall because I was knocked out cold. I woke up with my oldest brother's wife, my sister-in-law, taking care of me at home, nursing a gigantic knot on my forehead. I never rode that bike again.

To show you how willful I was, one day, my dad was

repairing the outdoor steps to our backyard at that same row house. I was almost seven years old then. He saw me coming near the steps and warned me not to come down until he finished. Well, I didn't like that command from him, so I looked down and saw the missing step.

I took another look at him and backed away. Now, you know me. The moment he stepped away to find the tool he needed, not only did I go down the steps, I decided to skip steps. My left leg was caught on the very nail that my dad clearly pointed out, and it stuck about one inch or more into my leg. That stopped me. I looked down and saw so much blood. But I didn't feel a thing. I guess my nerves went into instant shock due to the severity of the accident. What I did feel was fear of seeing so much blood and fear that my father caught me in the act of misbehaving.

Again, my sister-in-law took me up to her room and helped clean my leg. Later that day, Mom took over with cleaning the womb and trying to stop the bleeding. I needed stitches. Back then, we didn't have health insurance, so we didn't go to the hospital or see a doctor unless it was life threatening. Today, I wear the scar on my left leg about five inches beneath my knee, with great pride. It's a constant reminder for me to slow down and think about the consequences.

I was out of touch with my dad back then. He stood six feet tall with a big, booming voice to me. His voice was like the sound of thunder and always scared me. I thought he simply didn't like me, and the feeling was mutual.

One day, someone knocked at our front door, and I ran to the door, looking out the screened door and asked, "Who is it?"

The man said, "Tell your dad the rent man is here."

I didn't know what that meant, but I thought he was somebody my dad needed to see. So I ran with excitement and yelled to my dad, "The rent man is here! The rent man is here!"

My dad said, "Hush your mouth!" in a very angry voice.

I didn't know what I did or said that was wrong, but he hurt my feelings really bad that day. Looking back, I realize now that my dad might not have wanted the rent man to know where he was, much less right at home at that very moment, and there I was, innocently yelling and telling all of his business. That's one of those moments I'll always remember.

Back then, I thought my dad was the meanest man on earth. I wanted Superman to be my dad. That's right, Superman! I watched those old reruns of my hero every time it aired.

Months later, we moved to another home in the same city, but it was out of our current school district. My two younger brothers and I didn't want to change elementary schools, so we would take the city bus to school. I would dress warm and make sure I had my protective bandages—two of them—placed perfectly straight across my leg, covering a large open wound and a smaller one. That nail wound took about a year or more to heal. I wore those bandages and had extras because I didn't want the sore to get punctured. All that greenish-yellow pus would come oozing out.

On a very cold and snowy day, my brothers and I got off the city bus and made our way to school, but we arrived too early. We ran into the principal. I thought he was such a nice man.

But on this day, he asked us, "Where do you live?"

Not thinking, I blurted out the new home address, and

he politely took us to the office. I was in third grade, and my younger brothers were in second and first grade. We had to transfer to the school in walking distance that same day. We didn't like that at all. We were independent children, and I was the leader. I looked out for my two younger brothers, but on that day, it felt like I had failed them.

Finally we accepted our new community and the new school. My younger brother would sometimes get into trouble by playing with matches and taking coins from Mom's purse. I was in fourth grade when someone from the office came to get me out of class.

I'll never forget what he said, "You need to go home. Your house is on fire."

I was terrified. What a horrible thing to say to a child. They couldn't find my younger brother, but they did find my baby brother. What was a child supposed to do with that kind of information? We walked home and saw the house in flames and firefighters busy at work. My sisters and brothers were there, including my younger brother, all very sad, standing around outside while watching the house burn with flames coming out the windows. My oldest sister was able to save her red IBM Selectric typewriter. My parents were heartbroken.

We received assistance from Red Cross. They placed us in a hotel temporarily, but it was not very nice. Yet we were thankful to have a roof over our heads after the fire. At that hotel, my two younger brothers would get on their knees and whistle. The cockroaches would come running out every time. Ah, such pleasant memories.

We lived at that hotel for a little while. Luckily for us, my parents already had a home to move into in the suburbs. It was going to be their new daycare center, but we moved in as a family instead. We lived there for a while, and soon we were moving once again. I was still in the fourth grade when we moved yet again back to the city. This was a life-changing move for me because that was when I met my best friend.

At this point, I will introduce several special people in my life: Jacqueline, Jermaine, Bates, Andy, and Barron. I will go back and forth in the years when they first appear in my life. Some of the time periods may cross with another, just as it did way back then. Nonetheless, each played a major role in my development as a person. I will do my best to guide you through each period or era so it all adds up. Here goes!

Jacqueline

My best friend has been in my life since we were kids, more than fifty years ago. She has always been there for me through good times and especially through the tough periods. Jacqueline, JacQui for short, has never judged me, and that goes both ways. We were the same in that regard because neither of us likes conflict.

Yes, my nature back then was willful toward my dad, but not with my friend. We have been there for each other as children growing up, trying to understand where we fit in in the world. We grew up together in those silly teenager years while our bodies developed and when we began to notice boys. We had so many crushes on lots of handsome guys at school. We were there for each other when we didn't feel well and when we moved far away to the West Coast while in high school.

On some of those days, we didn't have lunch money. We were too proud to hang around at school feeling hungry, so we'd walk to a nearby neighborhood store that sold magazines. That kept us occupied the entire lunch period. She'd daydream and read about Shaun Cassidy, and I'd daydream and read about Parker Stevenson from *The Hardy Boys/Nancy Drew Mysteries*. We had such hard crushes on those two guys, so much so until we wanted them for our husbands. Yes, there's something special about young love. It comes and goes so quickly, like a new sunrise and sunset.

We helped to make each other's day with encouraging words to get up and go to school, study, practice modern dance, or do any other activity that we might neglect because we just didn't feel like going to school, practicing, or doing a particular activity at that time. We helped each other find jobs. We sometimes worked at the same location or other times not.

When we both found ourselves as mothers, we shared stories about our sons that helped shed light on many situations. She'd listen to my advice and would put certain things into action. I'd do the same after listening to her advice when the situation related to my son. We had our moments of being out of touch, but even though we didn't talk every single day—and still don't—we know that all we need to do is pick up the phone and call. We'd have a telephone visit that would sometimes last more than two hours. It became common.

When we spoke on the phone, it was an event. I preferred it that way because she was married and still lived in California. I was back east, still living at home. So I took it upon myself not to call too often because I knew how selfish or insecure some men can be when it comes to sharing time with their spouse with their best friend. Plus, I'd never been married, and I certainly didn't want to send negative karma into the universe to make its way back to me whenever that day came for me to say, "I do."

Back in 1997, I was her maid of honor at her second wedding, this time to John, and I was able to provide sound counsel to her that was beneficial for them. John is such a positively motivated man and a genuinely nice guy who deeply and sincerely loves JacQui. I believe they were made for each other, and they recently celebrated their twentieth anniversary. They're still going strong!

I love the fact that her husband has absolutely, positively no problem with us on the phone or when we're together. If John's around while we're acting silly, he'll sometimes jump in and go right along with us! They have always made me feel comfortable while visiting in their home. Of course, my visits have been scarce, but when I'm there, I have such a good time with both of them. I am humbled and thankful to have held on to a friendship for all these years.

We were kids when we met back in 1969. We were next-door neighbors. She was in the fourth grade, and I was in the fifth. We attended the same elementary school. Her family was there before we moved right next door. So I was the outsider. I would watch her play on the front porch with her sisters and other neighborhood friends with Barbie dolls. I thought, *Wow! Who wants to play with that? Dolls? That's so boring.*

I never liked dolls. When she wasn't playing with those

Barbies, we played together and always had a lot of fun. Once we finally became friends, she taught me how to play hopscotch and how to shuffle a deck of playing cards, and I loved doing both, especially shuffling the playing cards. We always had to hide the cards if my parents came around because they didn't allow us to play with them. We became inseparable little friends, and we wanted to spend the night at each other's home. Our moms said it was okay, but it turned out that JacQui would end up staying at our house more than I spent the night at hers.

My parents were seriously into church. Dad was a minister and pastor, and Mom was an evangelist. The pastor's kids were the church choir called the *Grant Specials.* Oh brother! Dad gave us that name. Anyway, the choir was made up of my three older sisters, one older brother, two younger brothers, and me. That made seven of us. My oldest sister was the choir director, and I led a few songs, from age seven through around eleven. I could sing pretty good back then.

There was an elderly man whom my dad would pick up for church. He loved to hear me sing. He would stand, scream, and clap his hands, and he was really happy. I felt good seeing him so happy because I felt sorry for him. He was a burn victim, and his face was a bit deformed from that trauma, as well as other parts of his upper body.

After church service, he would look down at me and say, "You are a very special little girl." He would say that almost every time he heard me sing.

As I was growing up, I heard that I was born with a veil over my face and never knew what that really meant. We grew up in the Holiness faith, and my dad preached from the Old Testament. He preached about fire and brimstone from the New Testaments of the King James Bible, which scared me a lot every time he preached about anything in Revelations, the last chapter in the Bible.

As a child with a vivid imagination, I'd sit there, listening and visualizing every word he said. If you know about Revelations, you know exactly what I'm talking about. I always thought it was a poor choice of words for the Bible to end with, "The End." Again, in my mind, I'm seeing that woeful, hot, chaotic ending with creatures who sting and everything else. Ugh!

JacQui's family dynamics were different than mine. She was the oldest child of seven who grew up with a single mom doing the best she could. Another family was living in the same household. I never noticed a dad around, so I guess they too were from a single-family home. From my point of view, there was always lots of fun things happing at their house next door, playing nice, loud music by Donna Summer and children having fun playing together with lots of joy and laughter. Her family sometimes struggled, which gave her that extra determination to be great at whatever she set her mind to be or do. She dreamed of becoming a successful businesswoman, which came true. She's that today, among many other great things.

My mother knew I was a lonely child. Yes, I'd play and have fun with neighborhood children, but while in the house, she could feel my sadness that ran deep. Back then in the early 1970s, I didn't realize the negative impact my sadness as a child would create for JacQui's siblings. As decades passed, I learned that they began to resent me for never inviting them over to spend the night too. Also, from their point of view, it seemed as though I took their big sister away from them. Wow, that's a tough pill to swallow.

Not only was I a sad little girl, I could feel spirits. I never liked the dark because I could feel them all around me. Sometimes while walking up the stairs, it would feel like they would try to pull me back toward them. No, I didn't really feel them touching me, but I did feel them deep in my soul. I would break out in goose bumps when that happened. Growing up as a young teenager and when JacQui wasn't there, I'd be afraid in my bedroom alone at night because it felt like there was someone else or others in the room.

During those days, we didn't have televisions in bedrooms. So the darkness didn't help, and I'd sleep with my head under the covers each night. I was too afraid to open my eyes to see who or what might be standing over me. Luckily I had a radio by my bed, and I slept with it on every night. I was in my mid-teens and distinctly remember Paul Simon's "Fifty Ways to Leave Your Lover." For some reason, music alone would help me to feel better. I'd pray to fall asleep before the song ended.

Then there was the Eagles' "Hotel California," which gave me the opposite effect, great fear and anxiety. I'd spring from my covers to reach the radio volume button to turn it all the way down and quickly cover up again before it got me. I needed music or something to take my mind off the unknown for the noise factor. I simply could not sleep in total quiet.

Finally I'd literally guess when another song was playing, and I'd go through the motions of turning the volume back up again. Yes, back then I was a big chicken! I was older then and in high school, but the eerie feelings never left me. Since I didn't understand what I was feeling, I decided that it scared me and it couldn't be good for me. I pushed it away deep inside and forgot about it. Or so I thought.

On some days, JacQui and I used to dress alike for school, and we used to laugh and talk a whole lot about boys. Yes, we were silly little girls growing up in two different worlds at the same time because of our different backgrounds. We would play the Jackson 5 albums so much that her mom took us to see them when they came to town. I was blown away and loved every moment of that show.

JacQui was sometimes moody, and I always knew when to give her space and time to herself and leave her be on certain days. I could sense she was sad about things, but I didn't know what to say or how to reach her then. I thought the best thing was to simply give her breathing room. She appreciated that space every time.

Fast-forward, my older sisters would go to the supper clubs in the big city. I was so upset when they'd leave because I wanted to go so badly. JacQui and I were in high school and thought we were grown. We'd play the albums and records of all the singing groups they saw and wish we were old enough to join them.

One day, my oldest sister said, "I'll take you two with us."

My oldest sister always has a plan in mind. Oh my goodness, that was music to my ears! We got permission from Jacqueline's and my mom. Both said it was fine because we'd be out with my three older sisters. This was my sister's way of introducing us to the finer things in life so we'd know the difference when we started dating.

JacQui and I could dance really well. Oh yeah, we had it going on! We were called up on stage at a certain point of the show with this very popular group, and we would dance to their amazement as well as the audience's. That would happen each time they came to town.

One day, we were asked to travel with them up and down the East Coast. My mother said no immediately, and we never asked or mentioned this to JacQui's mom.

Later in October 1977, I was a senior in high school. My two older sisters, my best friend, and I decided to move to California to be with my oldest sister, who was married then. My oldest sister had two young children, and we loved being close to them. My niece and nephew were very young when they all moved to Northern California, and I missed my little niece and little nephew really bad. We missed our big sister too, so we drove from the East Coast to California. It took several days on the road to finally reach our destination.

I didn't like living on the West Coast too much. I really missed being home on the East Coast, and I especially missed my mom. JacQui and I went to the local high school on the West Coast from October through December of 1977. It took a while before we finally accepted our new life in California and the high school. Sometimes I drove my sister's brand-new canary yellow Pontiac Firebird. Oh, how I loved driving that car!

We were something else over there. We also took a modern dance class, and I put together a dance routine. We performed together to Shaun Cassidy's "That's Rock 'n' Roll." We had a great performance that December 1977, but I was homesick and missed my mom. JacQui and I decided to take the bus home for the holidays. We spent four days on Greyhound.

When we arrived, JacQui went home to her mom, brothers, and sisters. I was super glad to be back home with my mom and the rest of my family too. We never went back to our high school in California. In January 1978, I enrolled in a Maryland high school, and JacQui enrolled in a DC high school. We went our separate ways at that point, and we stayed in touch, of course.

So near the end of my final high school year, I remember how each of my friends would say which college they were going to after leaving high school. I felt so bad because I couldn't say that I was going to college ... period. I did say that I was going back to California, but this time I'd go to the southern area.

I mentioned this to one of the members of the popular singing group we danced for, who was also curious about what we'd do after high school. I told him we were moving to Southern California. He said he could help us get a job because a dear friend of his owned a restaurant there. I thought that was the best news for us because we'd already have a job when we arrived. That was indeed the one and only time I had a job hookup.

I graduated from high school on the East Coast in early June 1978. The next month, my older brother was murdered, and the entire family, especially his wife and two young daughters, were in shock by his sudden death. He was robbed at a popular bank. My brother was a successful businessman and entrepreneur, and he was there to withdraw cash for a portion of his payroll.

To make a long story short, a group of people was securing jobs in the area whose sole purpose was to find out about payroll day and how it was handled. If a business were found to handle cash, they were robbed. My brother found out about the planned robbery when he fired his secretary, who was one of the crew. My brother told the police what was planned, and they believed him because of the other robberies. The police department allowed him to be his own decoy.

On that fateful day, he wore a bulletproof vest for protection. Plainclothes and uniformed police were there too, but the triggerman shot him in the throat, blowing out his vocal cords, and my brother choked on his own blood.

Later that summer, JacQui and I decided it was time to go on back to California. Remember, the friend who gave us a job hookup? Well, that worked out until the restaurant burned down. I'll never forget how much I loved working in the restaurant business. JacQui worked the breakfast and early lunch shifts, and I handled the lunch and dinner shifts. It was always nice when our shifts crossed.

Lunch was the busiest shift, and we handled the lunch rush with ease. The owner trusted me to make daily bank deposits, and I'd drive her car to buy wholesale meats. I'd tally up the register drawer each night and balance the meal sales tickets against the cash and checks received. I was also expected to manage that restaurant since the owner had plans to expand by opening a new one in Beverly Hills. We were riding high and had catering contracts to provide meals for two popular shows, *The Jeffersons* and *Diff'rent Strokes*.

But all that came to a sudden end with the fire. Yes, the restaurant burned down to nothing. That was the second fire in my life. Both were very devastating. We decided to stay in California and moved up north once again to be with my oldest sister, her husband, and my niece and nephew.

It took a while for us to settle in and find jobs. JacQui and I tried to join the military, the air force. We both signed up one day and were happy. The next thing I knew, the recruiter took several of us to a base for testing and our physical. Neither of us got in. It felt like a smack in the face because I come from a sort of military family. My dad was in the army and a proud World War II veteran. My older sister served in the Women's Army Corp. My older brother in the second family served in the air force, and my baby brother served in the army.

The angels have a way of not allowing certain things to happen. That makes twice when I thought I was on a roll that things didn't work out for me—the restaurant and military— because it wasn't meant to be. I was supposed to keep moving right along in Northern California so I'd meet the man who would become my son's father.

Those were the good ol' days, until I learned that I took many things for granted and never gave thought to how JacQui felt about her new life with our family. Recently she shared with me that she thought I was very selfish in my younger years and that I always wanted more. I was shocked and taken aback. She said I took for granted that I lived with my parents and we had a good life. She also reminded me that I was the only one in the neighborhood who lived with her mom and dad.

After I took that hit in the gut, I recomposed myself and continued listening. After hearing her—I mean really hearing her say those words to me—I said, "The thought of you not living with *both* parents never occurred to me. I too was a child, and from my point of view, my life was the only one I knew. Maybe it seemed like I wanted more because, back then, my older sisters were buying my school clothes and the like, and they made it perfectly clear that I had to share what I would have gotten with you."

I never told her until now, and she saw things a little differently as well. She understood why I seemed to always want more. We were in grade school and our early teens during those years of sharing, but I had no problem divvying everything with her. She was the little sister I never had. We're both adults now. We talked it out, and our friendship is stronger for it.

Her real siblings did not appreciate the fact that I took JacQui from them. It turns out that she would spend the night and never want to go home. She'd be in tears when it was time for us to take her home from being with us over the weekend. That was during the days when we moved back to Maryland and were no longer next-door neighbors. Her tears made everybody feel sad, and we'd sometimes cry with her. My older sisters would think of reasons for why she needed to stay, and then they would call her mom to get permission.

But JacQui's younger brothers and sisters didn't know she never wanted to go back home. They didn't know how badly we felt dropping her off and how we were all in tears when we did. Nonetheless, that resentment toward me exists to this very day. I can only say that I'm sorry for all the pain and hurt our friendship has caused them over the years. I take full responsibility for not including her siblings when perhaps there might have been times I could have. I was a child too, and my thoughts were on having fun with my best friend. I was already stretching the fact that I was playing with someone a whole year younger than I was. I simply never thought about how her younger sisters and brothers felt left out.

I finally let go of that guilt because I realize it was not intentional and Source knows my heart. Today, JacQui enjoys a wonderful life in Northern California with her loving husband, as well as a very close relationship with her son, mother, sisters, and brothers.

Jermaine

In 1976, I met a very handsome, loving guy who went to the same high school as I did on the East Coast. After he graduated from high school, both of us worked at the same mall. He sold shoes from a fine shoe store, and I sold neatly folded clothes for the latest in cool jeans. He was just a year older than I was, with fine character; muscles; big, beautiful legs; bright eyes; and soft curly hair. And he was well endowed. He knew how to handle himself, if you know what I mean!

He gave me permission to drive myself home from work with his car, something he never did, because he really loved his car. I couldn't wait to pick him up from work. We became very close, but things didn't work out because there would be periods of time that seemed like he dropped off the face of the earth. He'd suddenly disappear ... and poof! He'd show up again.

I became fed up with his comings and goings and had a serious talk with him about our relationship. I felt that I was in it all alone, but he couldn't see that. I thought, *Enough is enough!* That was around the time I left the East Coast for the first time, which was in October 1977. I didn't tell him I was leaving. I moved to California to live with my oldest sister and her family. I called Jermaine from there, to tell him that I had literally moved on from our relationship and away from him because he could not seem to get himself together as a young man. He seemed to always have a problem of some kind that he was dealing with, and I was simply tired of going through those changes. I loved him and wanted him in my life, but he wasn't ready, and I was ready for more. We would find each other again many years later.

Bates

After my high school graduation and my brother's untimely death, I was living in Los Angeles, working at the restaurant. I can't remember exactly when the restaurant burned down, but it was somewhere during the spring or early summer that JacQui and I decided to move back up north to be with my oldest sister. I knew I needed to move after working just a half-day in a warehouse that packaged blue jeans for shipment. I could hardly bear the smell of all the dye in the jeans. It literally made me sick to my stomach. I gagged practically all morning and fought to hold back from puking all over those damned jeans. The smell in that place gave me a headache.

When JacQui and I went to lunch, I said, "We can't go back in there. Let's quit!"

She agreed, so we moved up north to live with my oldest sister and her family in Northern California. She had just moved there in August 1980. That summer, my older brother, his wife, and one of my older sisters who lived in Los Angeles came up to visit with us. We went out to a club called Wine and Roses and enjoyed ourselves.

That night, I met the most handsome guy, Bates. He had such a beautiful smile and a very nice, thick beard that I loved. He was in shape and wore his jeans well, outlining beautifully shaped legs. We danced all night and had a great time. We became close friends. We both worked in the same big city and caught the subway, or Bay Area Rapid Transit (BART), to work.

My sister paid for our mom to fly out for a Christmas visit during the holiday season and to bring in the new year of 1981 with us. Bates's spirit never resonated with my mom from the moment they met, which meant he was not the one for me. I was only twenty-one, and I didn't listen to her because I really liked him a lot. Plus, I didn't know that my mother was very intuitive. Anyway, we took family pictures while she was there because we wanted to hold on to those beautiful memories.

A couple months later, I found out that I was pregnant with Bates's child. I had my son and found myself in the role of a single mom. I was from a strict family background. Both parents were ministers. I felt like I embarrassed the entire family for having a child out of wedlock. I quickly got over that because of the love I received from all my family for the both of us. I made a promise to Bates that I would do both parental parts so our son would live a happy life without him.

You see, Bates was a man with great ambition and the gift of gab, but he also had a knack for attracting trouble. Although he was handsome and very fit, he simply couldn't find his way to his life's path. Looking back, I realize he was caught up in the lower frequencies, and they had him right where they wanted him, in their control.

I decided to move back home to be with my parents on the East Coast in 1982. I knew I needed a fresh start for my son and myself, especially after Bates and I were through. I missed all my sisters who were still either in Southern or Northern California at the time. I would chat on the phone with my oldest sister, who was about to start a business there. I reminded her that all of the major organizations related to her business idea were here in Washington, DC. She thought about it and convinced my other two sisters to join the business. The four sisters were all together again.

In 1983, we launched a family business. My oldest sister was the president, my older sister was the executive vice president, another sister was vice president, and I too was vice president. Our family business had us attending various meetings as we tried to grow the business. I needed a stage manager for a project that my sisters and I coordinated each year.

It was around this time when Jermaine and I found each other again. I asked if he would be the stage manager, and he agreed. The contract required that we put together a formal Friday night dinner and a parade and two outdoor simultaneous festivals the next day. We did that for more than ten years.

My role was the director of entertainment, and Jermaine

was a person I could rely on to manage the larger of the two stages. That put us back into each other's lives, but it didn't work again. He saw life much differently than I did. I tried to help him as much as I could, but I ended up losing myself instead. When I realized what was happening again, I ended the relationship for good this time. We parted as friends.

Years kept ticking away. In the mid-1990s, my son insisted on meeting his dad. I took him on a trip just for that. They tried to keep in touch, but that didn't last very long because Bates just couldn't hang in there. They never bonded or established any type of a relationship. All I wanted was to make my life right. I wanted my family to be together. I wanted to be a wife to my son's dad, and I longed for us to be a solid family. That was a very sad time in my life.

Deep down inside, I knew my mom was right when she said, "He is not the one for you" when she first met Bates in California. I suddenly realized that it would always be just the two of us. Bates would never be a part of our lives again.

Andy

In the latter half of the 1980s, I met a wonderful man, Andy, at a business meeting. He was a professional with a high position in his company. Andy was a very handsome older man who exuded sophistication. He was fifteen years older than I was. My young, naïve eyes saw him as a man with real character. I didn't think he'd like me, but he did.

At first, I felt so insecure and thought I wasn't good enough or not in the same league to be with him. That was my low self-esteem talking. Our first date was really scary. We went downtown to a hotel suite of one of his longtime friends who was in town on business. He had several friends there visiting with him. I would listen to the conversations, not adding much or nothing at all. I spent the entire evening hoping and praying that they wouldn't ask me a question of any kind. I just didn't want to participate in their conversation. I was happy to sip on my glass of red wine. I made it through that evening, and I was so relieved when we left to go home. I could finally breathe again.

Andy and I became an item, or so I thought. In hindsight, it's almost funny how I allowed this whole situation to unfold. He told me right from the beginning that he dated other women and that he would not change. I didn't believe him and foolishly thought, *I can change you to want only me.*

I was a single mom, and my son was in elementary school at the time. I went on with this relationship for eight years. It ended badly. But before all that and when we first got together, I asked him why he was interested in me because he could have just about any woman he wanted.

He said, "I like you. You're my project."

The word *project* made me feel some kind of way or like Elly Mae Clampett from *The Beverly Hillbillies.* Elly Mae was an unsophisticated tomboy who spoke with a great Southern drawl. She was beautiful on the outside with a great body, but she lacked in etiquette and sophistication because of her humble Southern roots.

At the time, I didn't understand exactly what he meant by "You're my project," but I knew I didn't like the sound of it.

That was why Elly Mae popped into my mind. I suddenly felt so out of place in a new world I knew nothing about.

Life went on, and I was swamped in debt. My bills followed me down the street and yelled my name out loud from nearby and from around the corner, asking, "Remember me? Remember us?"

Andy knew that my credit score couldn't get any lower. He offered to help and suggested that I sign up for a secured credit card to start a path to rebuild my credit. Well, coming back from a terrible credit score proved to be a bigger challenge than either of us anticipated. I mailed the application for a secured credit card account, along with a $300 check, as that amount would be my secured credit limit. I would be charging against the funds that I sent to open the account, so there was no risk at all to the bank.

I was looking forward to that secured credit card, and after about ten days passed, I would check the mail for the new card every day. I finally got a response, but it was a letter and not the secured credit card. They sent the check back, and the letter meant, "Thanks, but no thanks." They refused to trust me with my own money. That was a new low. I'll never ever forget that for as long as I live.

Andy was kind enough to take me on trips out of town, dinner, and other entertainment. He paid every time because he knew I was in a struggling small business. He would ask all the time, "Why don't you get out of that stuff and find a real job?"

I'd look at him, thinking, *You just don't understand.* He kept saying this until one day it worked. I decided to get a job while remaining part of the business to tackle my bills and get on track with my finances.

We lived in a nuclear family home arrangement at the time in Maryland. My parents lived there, along with all my sisters, my niece, two nephews, and my son. The house was overflowing with love and excitement. We worked hard to pay the bills at our business and home. We'd gather every morning at the kitchen table with our mother. We'd talk about the day and what we were working on while sipping on the best coffee that she made, and sometimes we'd have a hot breakfast with homemade biscuits and home-fried potatoes with onion, bacon, and cooked spiced apples. We were on our own if we wanted eggs. Mom would only fix the entire plate for Dad. Nobody cooks better than my mom! Yes, those were the good ol' days. I really miss that time in my life.

While living at that house, I felt things like spirits. I'd shrug it off and continue on with my life. We'd get to work, and I could feel something there too. Sometimes we all would feel or see something that swiftly passed by or hear something strange, and we'd look at each other and ask "Did you see that?" or "Did you hear that?"

We would get up really quick and head straight for the door to go home. We didn't mess around with haunts, spooks, or ghosts. At least that was what we thought they were. We knew we could work from home at any time since we were the business owners. It was great when we landed our first government contract. We trained disenfranchised students to become office workers. We taught them how to type, along with old-fashioned Gregg Shorthand writing. I taught both classes. The main subject was positive thinking and motivation, taught by my oldest sister. We'd also teach them how to write their own résumé and how to put together and execute their very own job campaign.

Back then, we didn't have online applications. We looked for jobs the hard way by going through newspaper want ads, searching through business journals and the like. In addition, we were awarded a federal grant for training. That was a big relief because our city contract was not renewed. Before our contract days, we'd type midterm papers for students and dissertations for many of the local college kids. It was back in the mid-1980s through the early 1990s when paying for typing services was very popular. I remember once when we were so happy to get a customer paying in cash for an inexpensive typed paper because that became our lunch money for the day. It's tough being an entrepreneur, and each day can be very different.

The company that Andy worked for supported the annual event that we coordinated all those years. He also represented his company at many events throughout the region. One day, while attending one of those snobbish events with him, I wore a skirt above my knees because I do have nice-looking legs in silk pantyhose and Andy loved my legs. I felt proud of my outfit. We spotted our table, and Andy pulled out my chair and held out his hand to help me to get seated.

I took his hand and prepared to sit. Well, much to my surprise, the material of my skirt and the slickness from my pantyhose met the material of the seat and created a slippery effect, so much so that I slipped right off the chair and landed on the floor. I could not stop myself from sitting. Yep, I landed right on the floor, and I was really embarrassed, one of my most embarrassing public moments in my life.

Everyone at the table saw what happened because Andy tried to catch me. I sat there for the rest of the evening feeling like Fred Flintstone when he'd get embarrassed and would shrink to nearly twelve inches tall in his seat. Yes, that's a moment I will never forget.

Back at Andy's place, I didn't like getting up in the night because of spirits. There were lots of them in his house. I just ignored my feelings as the spirits remained there. It was always the same thing. While going to tinkle in the night or walking up the steps, I could feel the spirits trying to get me to come back down to them.

In 1995, Andy and I took a trip to an island. I couldn't swim, but I learned how to swim during that trip. He was very patient, and he taught me the basics. Andy would always warn me, "Don't go out too far because you need that same energy to swim back from that distance."

One morning, we were having a great time out in that big, beautiful ocean. Suddenly I looked around and dashed out of the water because I thought I saw a shark. The water was so clean and clear. It turns out that I dashed away from my own shadow.

Andy just laughed and laughed at me and even imitated me coming out of the water. I must admit that it really was funny once I got over the embarrassment. On our last day of swimming in the ocean, we swam out farther than previous days. We had been building up our stamina. Oh boy, did we both get tired on the way back. I thought to myself, *Why can't*

I feel the bottom of the ocean? When will I get close enough to wade in the water the rest of the way to the beach?

Swimming suddenly became very difficult. Andy saw that I was exhausted. I was panicking and fighting the water. My energy level was low.

He said, "Keep your head up out of the water, and try not to panic by moving too much!"

I checked to feel for the bottom of the ocean one last time. I didn't feel anything and thought, *This is it. I will drown today.*

With all his might, Andy helped me to keep from going under. Suddenly I felt the sand beneath my feet. We were close enough for both of us to wade in the water. We were exhausted and finally made it back to the beach. We sat there and caught our breath. Everything became very quiet. We looked out at the big, beautiful, powerful ocean that had just beaten us both to a pulp. To this day, we have never discussed that day on the beach.

Andy and I had a special relationship because we actually liked each other. We made each other laugh, and we became close friends. At least that was what I thought.

One day out of the blue, he said to me, "I'm tired of doing everything."

In shock, I looked at him. "What do you mean by that?"

He explained, "I'm tired of paying for literally everything."

"Okay. From now on, you won't have to pay for anything for me."

I went home feeling very hurt. I guess he must have compared me to one of his other women who had lots of money and could afford many things. To me, that ended our relationship because

I couldn't believe he would throw the lack of ready cash in my face. I thought that was a low blow and a deal breaker. I stopped seeing him, but he wouldn't give up.

I was too hurt and ready to accept the fact that our relationship would go nowhere. I listened to a classic sung by Bob Marley and the Wailers, "Waiting in Vain," every chance I could. For some reason, the song fit our relationship, and the sound of Bob Marley's voice was very soothing.

Months later, he found a way to win me over, and I was back in his life once again. This time, I thought I was making real progress, but he never paid for everything ever again. If I couldn't afford to pay my way for travel or an event, I simply wouldn't go.

One year, his mom was in town for his birthday. She was a very nice woman, and we really got along well. After a great birthday dinner, we were all sitting together in the living room having a great discussion, and his mom said he needed to settle down.

She asked him, "Who will you marry?"

I thought that was a very bold question to ask, especially in front of me. His mom and I both thought he'd say me, but to both our surprise and while I was sitting on his lap, he said someone else's name. That was the end of my eight years with this older man. I was so deeply hurt.

At home, I listened to Toni Braxton's Grammy Award-winning hit, "Breathe Again." Even though that song was a few years old by then, I couldn't help but listen to it over and over again. That song helped me get through a very rough time in my life and allowed me to sit day after day in my own private pity party. Eventually the song helped me to know that I wasn't the only one out there facing the end of a devastating breakup. And once the fog burned off, I thought, *I will never be with another older man again.*

Andy taught me a great lesson in survival: always believe what a man says out of his mouth the first time he says it. He told me right from the beginning that he would not stop dating other women. Why didn't I believe that? I was young and naïve while he was much older and experienced. I actually thought I could change him to settle down and become committed to only me.

It took many years, nearly a decade, for me to forgive Andy. That type of hurt and pain is slow to wear off because of so many great memories coupled with what I thought was our friendship.

We are finally friends again. I am so grateful to him for instilling deeply rooted values that led to my independence. His words, "I'm tired of doing everything," turned me into the independent woman I am today, and I'm very proud of myself for having great character and unwavering values. I owe much of that to Andy's abrupt wake-up call to me. The world is different today than it was in my parents' day. Back then, couples got married. Nowadays, couples spend lots of time together at each other's place, or they move in together, share costs on dates, travel, and entertainment.

Andy could not have made that point any clearer. I never ask for help, but my family and friends all know that, if I ask for anything, I must really need it. They also know that they would never have to find me to pay them back. Both my independence and my word means the world to me. I feel blessed that I have the discipline to manage money in a manner that works well for me. Without Andy's comment, I don't know if I would have ever developed such discipline.

Although I haven't seen him in person since we split toward the late 1990s, Andy and I do have friendly conversations over the phone, and we send emails and text messages to each other just to keep in touch. It took a long time for me to finally forgive him for simply being himself. I finally forgave myself too for being so foolish. I'm really glad that I let go of all that anger. I realize now that Andy did what I allowed.

Life really does get better when you find alignment. But for me, believe it or not, I had even more of this same lesson to learn. Who knew that I still needed to learn how to really hear a man and what he says the first time he says it?

Barron

Time spent with Barron is the final chapter of my life before relocating to Arizona. Everything culminated and came to an end—some things dramatic, but endings all the same. Life went on, and the years seemed to speed by.

One day back in the early 2000s, I went to a seminar at work and saw the most handsome guy conducting the meeting. I found myself totally captivated, and I simply had to meet him. I realize now that the universe sent this test following some years after my lesson with Andy, and I failed miserably. Not only was he another older guy, fifteen years older than I was, but I betrayed myself by getting involved with a much older man again.

He said to me the very first month together, "I'm not looking for a relationship."

I thought to myself, *Hmm, that's a weird thing to say. Wonder what compelled him to say that.* Then I pondered, *I'm ready for a relationship, and I'm gonna change your mind.*

Why couldn't I hear him the first month we met? Here I went again, thinking that I could change his mind and he'd choose me to be his wife. That never happened. It's like hearing Judge Judy ask a defendant or claimant when she surmises that something isn't quite right in his or her understanding department. She asks, "Are you thick?"

I won't go into everything, but our relationship lasted twice as long as my relationship with Andy did. We were together for sixteen years, and I have nothing to show for it except for a boat with red sails on my shelf and the fact that we are still friends.

We met in April 2000 and soon became a couple, companions if you will. I helped him through depression from having his dog put down, and he supported me mentally with my travels back and forth to see my very sick mom. I'd drive down south nearly every weekend to visit her and my two sisters who moved there to help take care of her. Mom had diabetes and amputated legs. She went to kidney dialysis and had high blood pressure, and she suffered from several mini strokes.

That year, I went home for Christmas holiday because she was not doing well. She passed away at 4:30 early Christmas morning of 2000. My older sister received the call from Dad, who was with her at the hospital when she left us. Thank God she didn't leave this world alone. My older sister and I got dressed and went to the hospital to see our mom. She was propped up on a pillow. I remember thinking how small she looked because she had no legs. I rubbed her forehead and the hair on her head and then gave her a kiss. She was still warm and not stiff.

I looked back, seeing my dad wearing a big black cowboy hat. He was sitting there in a daze with his legs crossed while staring out the window. He looked at us and said, "My partner's gone, y'all."

I knew he felt lost and so alone because I could hear it in his voice and saw that look in his eyes. They'd been together for over fifty years. She was his lifeline, and he was certainly hers. I felt deep sadness and missed her so much already, but I felt so sorry for Dad. He was sad. Everything changed when Mom passed away.

Before I left to come home for that Christmas holiday, I told my employer I would be down south and would be back to work right after New Year's Day. When our mom passed away, my sisters and I found ourselves in a situation. I needed to extend my stay and help with funeral arrangements. I contacted my employer, who was fine at first but then angered me beyond words when I received an email asking if I would come back to work the week after her funeral.

I realize that, in most other cases, the employer was not being unreasonable. But when you're grieving for your mother, no one should direct you to come back to work. I thought that was heartless. January rolled around, and I went back to work right away, but you know me, I was hot under the collar, and I had to leave that job. There was no way I'd continue working there, feeling the way I did. On one hand, I was very unhappy at work. On the other hand, I was glad I had a job because I wanted to become a homeowner.

Barron was there for me and supporting me during the last year of my mother's life. He also knew I wasn't happy living in an apartment. After coming back from Mom's funeral, he said I could move in with him. That way, I could save, get out of debt, and find a place that I really liked as a first-time homeowner. That was the plan.

My son had just graduated from high school in June 1999. He made plans to live with friends in a nearby city and would also enroll at the university they were attending. That whole year was very foggy in some respects. I accepted Barron's suggestion, and I moved in with him. I had never lived with a man before, and my son never lived without me. His plans to move in with friends seemed okay while I regrouped at Barron's and picked up the pieces of my life. Barron inspired me to save as much as possible and pay off bills so I could one day move into my own place.

I soon found a new job early in the year 2000 with the same employer. I had to get away from the office that rushed me back after my mother transitioned. I worked hard to make my job meaningful. Lord knows I needed that job badly because I was on a mission to become a homeowner.

I tested the water one day while Barron was with me. We went to a new development of townhomes, and I decided I wasn't quite ready because I didn't have enough saved for a down payment and the monthly payments would become a struggle. Furthermore, that development was right across the street from a lot of very large antennas, and I didn't know what those frequencies might do to the human body over a period of time. I moved past that and focused on work and my goal.

Meanwhile, it was the morning of September 11, 2001. There were several televisions in the lobby at my place of employment, and I saw an airplane hit one of the towers in New York. It was the first airplane to crash into the first tower of the World Trade Center. My initial thought was *How will the fire department put out that fire in such a tall building? How will a construction company fix that?*

Then suddenly another airplane crashed into the second tower. I was then glued to the television, along with a coworker. I knew something very bad was happening. Then we went back to our offices but kept a close ear to the news. Then it was reported that a third airplane crashed into the Pentagon, very close to our location. People began to panic and left the office for safety, wherever that was. Now a fourth airplane crashed near Shanksville, Pennsylvania. The courageous passengers and crew on that flight knew they were being hijacked and had heard about the other three airplane hijacks and crashes. So they took over and caused the crash, successfully thwarting the hijackers' fourth mission.

After I composed myself enough to think and snap out of the fear, I called my son to make sure he was okay. He was. I called Barron, and he had left the building he was working in, which was close to the Pentagon. He was walking to safety, wanting to reach his car. I'll never forget where I was that day. Barron and I stayed up all night watching PBS for authentic news.

That was a gloomy time in America and around the world. I believe that event was the beginning of our current shift we are now experiencing on Planet Earth. Months later, life eventually started to feel sort of normal again. President George W. Bush urged Americans to go out, travel, and simply live again. It was very hard to feel a sense of normalcy. And that day came when many people throughout the United States resumed everyday life, but nothing would ever be the same again.

Time ticked on, and I could never shake the feeling that Barron's house was haunted, especially in the basement. It was a very old house with one full bathroom on the upper level and a half bath on the lower lever, where the kitchen was. While sleeping on the top floor, I had to walk downstairs in the middle of the night to tinkle. It was uncomfortable, but I found a way to manage by waiting until the last minute, which allowed me to focus on tinkling and not the spirits. That only worked while going to the bathroom. When I was done, I always felt the spirits seemingly pulling at me from behind. The feeling of spirits hanging around never left me.

My move to Barron's home turned out to be a bad decision for my nineteen-year-old son. He had trouble settling down. I helped him whenever he reached out for assistance. It bothered Barron because he said, "He'll never grow up if you keep helping him every time he calls. He needs to learn to manage his own life."

Deep down inside, I knew he was absolutely right, but I still looked at him like he was the creature from the Black Lagoon. I'd think to myself, *Now I know you're not talking to me about my child.*

I'd just ignore him because I carried such a heavy burden of deep guilt for the change in my son's lifestyle. Once the fog settled and I saw how my son was actually handling life without me, it simply broke my heart. Barron said my son could not live in his house, so I did all I could and then some each and every time he needed any little thing. Yes, I became an enabler to help with my gigantic sense of guilt.

I was stuck. I felt great guilt because my son was suffering, and as his mother, I allowed that to happen when I decided to move in with Barron to work my plan of becoming a homeowner. Now I realize that I've connected those dots in the worst possible way, but that's how I felt at that time. What a burden to carry. Even to this day, it brings tears to my eyes when I think about his life back then.

One day out of the blue, back in September 2003, Barron asked me, "When are you going to move?" He can be surprisingly direct at times. It's just his personality.

I know he was merely asking a question and didn't mean any harm because that's not his nature, but my ears just didn't like the way those words parted from his lips. I looked at him and thought to myself, *I know you didn't just say that to me!*

He politely and very sincerely mentioned our plan, saying, "I haven't seen any activity."

I thought, *Oh boy, whatever compassion or understanding I had for his initial question is gone. It's on now!*

I calmly said to him, "I'm looking and will have a place soon."

I had been thinking about it but hadn't done one single thing toward making a move. Well, a couple weeks later, I found a real estate agent, and we started looking at properties. I was hurt that he mentioned it, but he was absolutely right to bring up that subject. Although I was working my plan to pay off bills, I had become complacent, along with feeling physically and mentally tired.

The places I could afford were all being sold to friends. I thought that was odd. So I ended up finding a place much farther out than I liked. My real estate agent was out of town when I found it.

One month after Barron asked about my moving plans, October 2003, I announced to him, "I found a place, and I'll be moving in March 2004 to a new development. I would be moving sooner, but my building is still under construction."

So it turns out that I wasn't angry with Barron; rather I was angry with myself for becoming complacent, which caused him to bring up the fact that I wasn't keeping up with the original plan: to pay off bills and then to save and become a first-time homeowner in the first place. I should have stayed on top of my game so the one person who helped me the most wouldn't have to ask about the plan.

Fast-forward, it felt good moving into my very own place. I thought, *I can't believe it! I'm a proud first-time homeowner of a condo on the top floor, the fourth floor!*

I was so happy, or at least I thought I was, that I was finally done with being the go-between with my real estate agent and the mortgage lender. I was happy because I won what felt like a battle from start to finish. But why wasn't I really happy or excited about my new place? Yes, on the surface, I was happy because the hard part was now over, and I had the keys to my new place. But deep down inside, I was still waiting to actually feel happy about my accomplishment. I worked so hard to clean up my credit, save money for my down payment, and find a place on my own. And when that day came that I was now in my own place, I kept waiting for the happiness that never kicked in.

I shared with my sisters and told them, "I'll be glad when it hits me that I'm a homeowner and can feel happy and excited about it."

But that day never came. I would think about all the changes I went through while being in the middle of a power struggle between my real estate agent and the mortgage lender. I acted as their intermediary and secretary and hated every minute of it. They would ask me to provide them with documents that they sent to me or a document to one or the other. That was extremely annoying. I've never liked conflict, and there I was, right in the middle of it. Then I recalled my reaction to Barron when he first asked about my moving status. I was simply embarrassed because I lost focus.

In December 2003, my new boss who joined the company late that summer noticed my hard work and dedication. He promoted me with a new position and additional salary. Things were looking really good at work. I was more comfortable in my new place because my budget had a little wiggle room with that promotion. I felt safe and secure at work too. I was finally in a place where I felt highly regarded and appreciated for my hard work.

Things were looking up, and on top of that, I had a very good boss. I was also being prepped to step into a senior position too. But in April 2004, my good boss resigned. I couldn't believe it. He had been there for only eight months. I thought to myself, *It takes nine months for a baby to form. He left in eight months.*

I don't know why that thought crossed my mind, but it did. I was in shock because I knew that new leadership meant great change in the office. In June, we met our new boss. Things were moving quickly, and in early July, she told me that my job would be abolished by the end of the month.

I was in shock again! I kept thinking that I had just bought a condo in March, a new boss had started late summer, and I had gotten a raise that December. I would think, *Happy days are here!*

The following year would give me scorpion stings. My nice boss left that April, the new boss started that June, and now I wouldn't have a job in July. What the hell? Oh, how I hated her with deep passion for causing me to endure such pain. She never worked with me before and didn't know me at all. She just didn't care. It was a business move. I understood that, but the sting really hurts when it affects every aspect of your life.

My angels are always guiding me, even when I work in a field I don't like. Back in February, right before my new boss left that April, I started fishing for another job with more pay. I had no reason to be searching because my future was looking so bright where I was. A good friend of mine told me that someone would be leaving a position in her department. She told me about the job and said the pay would be more. Then she asked if I were interested.

Not married to any of my jobs with this employer, I said, "Yes, I'm interested. Please keep me posted."

She said she would.

Now without a job, I pretended for my son's sake that everything was okay. He had no idea about any of this. At the time, he was a young adult, but he doesn't handle stress well, especially if he thinks something is not right in my life. He was finally doing fine now. He was living with his girlfriend, and that relationship was serious.

But suddenly things started to fall apart for them. He moved in with me that August. So I lived in my condo alone for only six months. Still carrying the guilt, I was more than happy for him to come back home.

Now that my son lived with me, I really had to put on a happy face since I had no job at all. I stayed in touch with my friend who mentioned the possibility of a job in her department, and it was true. I interviewed for the position and got the job. I landed on my feet yet again with the same employer. What a relief! I had a higher salary, and once again, I could pay all my bills and remain insured.

Life was feeling pretty good again, and my son was home. The whole family thought I did too much for him. I must admit that I did. I became the butt of jokes too. I was told that all he had to do was ask for anything and I'd say yes. They were right.

Nothing—and I mean nothing—could ever replace those few years he struggled on his own while I did the best I could to have a better life. It took many years to accept the fact that he turned out just fine and he is a well-adjusted young man who respects his elders and has real character. But at the same time, I was selfishly holding him back from being all that he could be. My guilt was strong. I was his enabler.

On my new job, just six months later, I was already bored with my day-to-day duties, so I happily started looking for another job. It takes time to actually find the job and move into a new position, so I just followed my heart and started looking once again. I thought, *Good grief! Why can't I be satisfied with where I work?*

It took no time for me to remember how I felt in my early teens—how I did not want an office job but did absolutely nothing to change my situation. My first position at this organization was in 1998. I started looking for another job just one week later. Oh my! That was a big sign from the angels right from the beginning with this employer. My angels were trying to get me to follow my heart. It turns out that I didn't have the passion to move on and find a career in the arts. I first needed to find my passion for what I really wanted to do with my life.

Since I was clueless about my passion, I decided to put that in my too-hard-to-do jar. So I stayed, and I was unhappy. And that's when hypertension set in, followed by hypothyroidism. I'd leave one job and get another just to move myself up and be challenged. I liked the newness and learning how to perform every new job. That kept me going.

As soon as I found my rhythm, it was time to look for something else. I learned a lot about the company because I had several viewpoints from working in so many different departments. I was an excellent and well-respected employee. It's just that the different positions paid more and helped me to keep growing as an employee as well as handling bills at home. But most of all, the different positions helped with my boredom from working in a meaningless office job in the first place.

Yes, I was coasting along in jobs that seemed as though I was excited about them, but they all turned out to be boring and meaningless. I did what I had to do to survive. I felt sad, broken, and unfulfilled. There I had job after job that was not aligned with me. On one hand, I felt I had something more to offer that would be a great help to others. But on the other hand, I was clueless as to what that was. I knew I had something inside to give, and I wondered a lot about what that could be.

I'd go home to a condo that for some reason I never could love. Perhaps it was because I was house poor during my first few months. I made enough money to pay all my bills on time every month, but that left practically nothing for groceries. At first, after all the bills were paid, I had twenty-five dollars left for the rest of the month. That turned out not to be as bad as it sounds. I survived. Remember, I was very resourceful at work, and during the times that I wasn't exactly changing positions there, I was getting annual and merit increases. So being house poor lasted no time at all.

After a while, life catches up with you. When it happened to me, I was worn out completely. I wondered, *Why does life have to be so hard? Why does everything I do feel like I'm constantly fighting an uphill battle?*

After I got over that, I created a whole new life on an Excel spreadsheet. There, I planned and calculated everything. Oh, that was exciting! I knew when to sell the condo, when to retire, when I'd be free from work, and when my student loan would be paid off. I loved watching the numbers from my retirement savings, stocks, and other accounts add up. I was managing my future like I'd be free from worry tomorrow. I was living in the future and totally ignoring the present.

That spreadsheet was my new life, and I simply loved it. It became my escape, and it provided comfort. I'd tweak it nearly every day, and through the night on weekends, it gave me hope and the willpower to continue. That spreadsheet helped me to deal with my lackluster jobs by showing me what I was working toward, a bright future.

Barron and I lived in different places, but we were still very much together. I'd be there on weekends and many times through the week. His home became my place of refuge, a home away from home. It felt good to be there because I wore the hat and the pants in my home and all the burden fell on me. It was the place where my son lived, where I'd look at him sometimes and still feel the guilt of him living unhappily for those few years right after Mom passed away. He was grieving back then because he loved and missed his grandma too. So the spreadsheet was all that I had to keep myself occupied and to step out of my reality. It took me away from all my problems and guilt.

Barron thought I was obsessed with my spreadsheets. He was right. I was. It was hard to put my laptop down. I monitored every bank account, savings, and all credit card accounts daily. I really didn't need bank statements because my accounts were reconciled to the penny daily on a spreadsheet.

I look back and see that was a dark time for me. I was very sad. I was determined to keep a high credit score because, in my mind, I felt like I was still pulling a heavy cross up a very steep hill. Each number on that spreadsheet represented a little bit of happiness and the life I dreamed of. It was all I had left to hold on to, and I wasn't about to let it go.

One day, I watched a PBS special and listened to Dr. Wayne Dyer. His words stuck out. "If you change the way you look at things, the things you look at change."

That statement really resonated with me. I started exercising by speed walking to snap out of my funk. I built up my stamina from a one-mile walk to two miles until I would walk five miles before work every other day during the week and five to twelve miles on weekends. I decided to focus on me in a positive way and get fit and healthy in the process.

I don't like to exercise, but I always feel so much better after a workout. Even Barron noticed the difference in my demeanor when I walked and when I didn't. It was very noticeable when I stopped for whatever reason because, in no time at all, that sadness would creep back in. The winter seasons always threw off my stride. I didn't walk if the temperature fell below freezing or thirty-two degrees. Getting fresh air and walking through the park trails and out in nature really helped my spirit. I took it a step further and bought outfits, sneakers, and other things that would boost my spirit to keep moving.

Yes, life was manageable, and I was content, but there was still a huge hole in my heart that would go unfulfilled. I decided to ignore that feeling and remain focused on what was working today, like my spreadsheet, a home ownership, employment with benefits, and my good health. The rest would take a backseat for my survival.

That went on year after year. I always found a way to hide my true feelings and maintain a great façade. It worked. It was easy, or so I thought until one day I had enough. I had no desire to exercise, go to work, and stay in my condo. I knew deep inside that all of this would change. Yes, I was depressed. The holiday season was fast approaching, and I was feeling some kind of way. I fell in love with the new hit by Jay-Z featuring Alicia Keys, "Empire State of Mind." I loved all the television appearances by her as she promoted her new song.

Barron and I usually celebrated the new year at home, sipping on champagne while watching Dick Clark. After the big celebration, Barron played more music, and he selected "Empire State of Mind" with Alicia Keys. He knew how much I loved that song. But for some reason tonight, the first hours of a new year (2010), I couldn't stop crying. The song had me in turmoil as I thought about my life.

If you listen to the lyrics, maybe you'd get some sense out of why the song so deeply touches my heart. It's all about the arts and how people can make it. I cried because I simply let my life pass me by. I wanted a career in the arts. I did nothing about it and worked in an office. I chained myself to what mattered at the time. Now my son manages his own life, and I was waking up and beginning to see that I was free. I was free all along.

That was a big nudge from my angels. My life was changing. Those tears were symbolic of so much to come. No, it wouldn't be easy, but I'd get through it. Deep down, I felt that my work life and daily life were coming to an end, but I had no idea how or when. There was something very strong stirring within me, and all I could do was feel my spirit freeing my mind. Things began to change. My tears were gone, and I was moving forward.

I snapped out of that depression once again and planned it all out in a different Excel spreadsheet. Yes, I do love my spreadsheets. This time, it was not for my future in a great distance, but rather it was for today. The angels were with me then, and they helped me every step of the way to make a plan to sell the condo in the spring of 2014 and begin to find myself. That was a mouthful. I could feel that I was on the verge of a new life. That fact excited me because I was up for a big change in my life, even if it meant moving to another state. I knew my plan for today would take a while, maybe a year or so, before things fall into place. But by now, I knew that things always worked out for me somehow. Why should this be any different?

In 2013, I could hardly believe that I had lived in my condo for nine years. But my divine plan would prove beneficial much sooner than expected. God (Infinite Intelligence or Source), all my guardian angels, my parents, my ancestors, and my higher self were with me all along. I still didn't realize it back then when I started working on my new plan for today.

Here's my angel-inspired plan. In the fall of 2013, I had a talk with my son, who was still living with me for nearly ten years. I told him to set a goal to move into his own place by January 2014 because my goal was to put the condo up for sale by the spring or April. I was ready to spread my wings and move to another state.

All of a sudden, I felt energized and rejuvenated just by that thought alone. At that time, I was looking at Connecticut or somewhere in New England. What loomed large in my mind was getting the condo ready for the market. Where would the extra money come from to replace carpet, painting, and so on? More importantly, how was I going to plan my move? That was a huge dilemma for me because I never did this before. I couldn't afford to move into an apartment in another state while my condo was on the market. That meant I would have to pay a mortgage and bills for the condo, plus pay rent and bills wherever I lived.

Geez! I thought, *Can a girl ever get a break?*

Deep down inside, I knew something would change for me. I didn't know what, when, where, or how, but I knew something good would happen.

During the holiday season of 2013, I was not in the mood for Thanksgiving, Christmas, or the thought of celebrating New Year's. I wanted change in my life. I'd been content with where I was for too long, and it was time to do something about it. I wanted to spend all my time focused on my new spreadsheet dealing with my future and the one for today. I didn't want to waste money on the holiday season because it would take away from my moving plans.

Anyway, I had to refocus and become enthusiastic enough to celebrate with my companion, Barron, whose lifelong friend would celebrate his seventieth birthday in Northern California. The trip was all set for our visit. We'd be leaving right after Christmas and returning the first week of January 2014.

I'd always have flashbacks to my relationship with Andy when it was time to travel or dine out. I always asked if I should pay for myself. I never wanted another man to ever tell me, like Andy once did, that he was tired of doing everything. I promised myself I'd never hear those words again from a man in this lifetime. I went on and planned our trip to bring in New Year's on the West Coast.

Meanwhile, in the days before Thanksgiving 2013, I called my oldest sister for advice about my job. I told her I was unhappy with this meaningless job. I couldn't see how I was helping others, much less feeling a sense of accomplishment for myself. She told me that I do help others because I see to it that vendors are paid, which helps their families and them. That was only one aspect of my job. I wore many hats, but none resonated with my spirit. My soul was starved, and I was determined to find nourishment.

In December 2013, I received a progress report from my son, who said that he had found a place and his move-in date was January 15. I was so happy for him! He was happy too, and I felt good about that. This time, he was moving and very happy about the progress he'd made in his life thus far. I could still feel some of the old guilt I had when he lived on his own and simply wasn't ready. But I realized I should put that out of my mind and focus on the present. Then I thought, *My plan is working. Hallelujah!*

Now it was time for me to figure out what I'd do about finding someplace else to live as well as the funds to get my condo ready for the market. I didn't dwell on it, and I prayed for a miracle and left it alone. But for the time being, Barron and I flew to Northern California for his friend's birthday celebration. That trip was just what I needed, a getaway. I love to travel because it always uplifts my spirit. I oftentimes wish I had enough money to see the world.

We brought in 2014 far away from the East Coast. It turned out to be a trip that I'll always remember.

As far as my job goes, I felt that I betrayed my natural instincts of wanting more freedom when it came to work. I knew as a young teenage girl that I wanted to travel and see the world and that I simply did not want to be in a stale office all day, attending boring meetings and then staring at a computer monitor. The arts were there all the time. The question is, "Why aren't I compelled or passionate enough to move into that field?"

In looking back, it is no surprise that the condo I found was rooted in negative power and energy. I reacted in haste because the one person who helped me the most, Barron, asked for an update on my moving plans. I went out in the world with a negative disposition right from the start. No wonder my realtor and loan officer could not get along. I created all that negative power and energy right from the beginning of my search. That was why everything seemed out of control between the real estate agent and the loan officer. That was why I never could feel at home.

I had to learn the hard way that I could never ever change a man's outlook on life. Always believe him the first time he utters any words from his mouth. I spent eight years in a relationship with Andy that went nowhere and followed that up with a marathon relationship of sixteen years that ended up nowhere with Barron. Both told me right from the beginning what they did or didn't want. I thought I could change them. I couldn't. Now my ears were ready to hear and receive. I listen to everyone. I had to live my life the way I chose to and experience all that I did in order to develop into the person I am today.

And that day came when I finally accepted the fact that I truly felt lost and so alone. No one knew. I had to keep a strong and happy appearance for my son, family, friends, and work family's sake. I took it one day at a time and often wondered, *Why was I ever born? No one should be this unhappy.*

I was stuck. I had no energy or desire to look for another position or to find another job. I thought I'd rather stay with the devil I know. If I only had passion for something else, I'd do something about it. I knew I was depressed again, but not so depressed that I couldn't get out of bed or do anything for myself. I was just very unhappy with my life. Yes, I knew that I accomplished a lot in my world. Yes, I was very proud of those accomplishments.

But I just couldn't shake the nagging feeling of emptiness, like there was a hole in my heart. I had given up on a life that could include travel, acting, dancing, and fun for a life that consisted of working in an office. But I knew there was so much more waiting for me elsewhere.

In reflection, I understand why it appeared that I was more aloof than ever. As a child, I couldn't understand my parents' struggles and their points of view when they moved from the South to the North. I was a very willful child, and it took a while for me to learn that there are always consequences for every action. Yes, I really learned that lesson well the day I rode my brother's bike into a brick wall.

Forty years later, I established a relationship with my dad that blossomed into something very beautiful. I'm glad we ended up with a strong and positive relationship. I inadvertently hurt my best friend's younger brothers and sisters because, in essence, I took her away from them. They missed out on many precious years of growing up together as siblings. I realize that it was nobody's fault one way or the other. I am more aware and in touch with who I am today than yesterday. Thank goodness I finally learned how to be true to myself.

Yes, it took me twenty-four years to finally get the message or to really hear a man's words the first time he utters them from his mouth. I can't think of a class in higher education that can outdo that kind of time to earn a degree, but I finally mastered that class. I'm also thankful I am more in tuned to other people's feelings. I am no longer aloof.

Chapter 2

Waterloo

Living in a Shattered World

It was a new year, a new day, and a brand-new way! Yahoo! Barron and I celebrated and brought in 2014 together in Northern California. We were here because one of Barron's lifelong friends would celebrate his seventieth birthday the first week of January. We attended the festivities and returned home to the East Coast on January 7 at his place. I was feeling anxious to get home because I'd been away since a few days before the last week of December.

Early the next morning—and still tired from the flight—my cell phone rang. It was about 4:30 a.m. It was my son. I knew immediately that it couldn't be good for him to call at this hour.

He told me, "Mom, the fire department is there, and our condo caused a huge flood throughout the building. You can even see the water poured out outside."

It was wintertime, and it was icy cold outside. The pipes

located in a room just off my balcony burst, causing the flood outside my building, throughout my unit, the unit beneath me, the unit beneath them, and so on into the lobby. What a way to bring in the new year.

I was devastated. I couldn't believe this was happening to me. After getting over the shock of that phone call with my son, I sprang into action. I hopped up and spoke with the foreman handling the cleanup. I contacted my insurance company to file a claim. I spoke with the emergency restoration company foreman for reassurance, the president of the condo association because he was on the scene, and the condo management company.

Barron said I could move back in with him. He really wanted to help because he was already worried about me before our trip. My mind was racing. I knew how much he loved having his space, and I didn't want to intrude again. My plan wasn't complete.

At that moment, I was vulnerable and simply defeated. With no other immediate choice, I gave in and accepted his offer.

Thank God my son was fine. He was staying at a hotel paid by my insurance company until his move to his own apartment on January 15. When I think about it, I find it amazing that I knew to prepare my son to move back in September. I asked him to be ready to move in January because I needed the time to start clearing things out and getting the place ready for market by spring. He enjoyed staying at the hotel until his place was ready.

You know I was extremely glad for him because his

happiness means the world to me. I'd like to point out how my angels were leading and guiding me through the whole disaster, starting with my son's move to his own apartment and then with Barron's offer to help.

I called the office to let my supervisor know what was happening. I even sent pictures from my phone to his email, showing the devastation. He understood and said yes to a few more days off to handle the emergency. Here, it was 2014, and I hadn't even been home or to work this year. I finally went home later that day when my son called about the emergency. I saw firsthand the terrible damage. It was shocking and a very ugly situation. The entire ceiling in the lobby had fallen down. There was no lighting in the lobby, except for construction site lights hanging around, and a few were positioned on the floor. Everything looked dark and grim.

I finally came to my unit and couldn't believe my eyes. It was truly a sad sight. Water damage appeared mainly on one side of the condo, the side where my son's bedroom and bathroom were located. The living room laminate floor was badly water damaged. I finally went to my suite, and there was water damage there too. That was a lot for me to take in.

The only place appearing undamaged was my bathroom. Everything else—my leather queen sofa bed set purchased less than six months ago, my son's clothes that were on the floor of his walk-in closet, the laundry room, and the kitchen floor—were all damaged. You get the picture. It was a big mess. I was tired and didn't want to deal with it.

But that little voice inside of me always told me to never

give up. So I looked up and asked God to give me strength. I became the little engine that could and started once again to coordinate face-to-face and on the phone in the evenings with so many other people now involved. Yes, it was another cross to bear, but "I think I can. I think I can."

Remember, I never went through anything like this before in my life. Drying floors and walls were extremely important for a successful outcome. I asked the foreman of the restoration company if the furniture were in the way of drying the floors and the walls. He said it was fine where it was. All the large pieces had been moved to the center of my wet living room. But the heavy-duty fans that the restoration company brought in were not getting the job done.

On January 15, I was at work and received a call that the floors weren't drying according to the floor drying plan and that I needed to move everything out as soon as possible. Now I was pissed because I had to rush and figure out a major move. I asked a week before if the furniture would be a problem, and he told me no.

I snapped out of that funk pretty quick and contacted my insurance company again, and they approved hiring a professional moving company on short notice because it was at the request of the restoration company. I took off work once again to help with the packing. I boxed up everything in the kitchen because I didn't want the movers in my kitchen packing anything. I had no help.

My son couldn't get off work, and Barron was at his house. This was not his problem. I found myself once again overwhelmed by the enormity of the entire situation. I couldn't believe this was happening to me. When I finally got over myself and the task at hand, I ended my pity party. Then I coordinated the packing with the moving company. They had many questions, and they were glad I was there to provide quick answers.

I was packing all the things in the kitchen in fast motion. I was running on adrenaline and like the little engine that could in motion. I have always lived by that theory because nothing ever seems to come easy for me. Hard work is all I know. This situation was no different. I had to jump in, figure out the problems, manage, coordinate, communicate, and get the job done. Yes, just get it done.

When I realized that there was no moving back into my condo and that a brief stay with Barron turned out to be indefinite, I accepted this as my fate and somehow found peace with it. I made arrangements to give away all my furniture that wasn't water damaged. The restoration company disposed all of the damaged furniture.

I began to think, *If I'm going through all this trouble to move everything out and I already had plans to put up the condo for sale in early spring, I would have no more concerns about what to do with my furniture. I'd simply be done with all of it.*

So while I was living with Barron, I arranged to give everything to family. Luckily my son received the keys to his apartment on the fifteenth because the movers were there the next day to move the furniture out of the condo to somewhere else. Most of the furniture was delivered to my son's place because it was empty. Oh my goodness, how things started falling into place. I suddenly stopped feeling sorry for myself and began to see this as a blessing. I was in the midst of a miracle!

It turns out that the money I didn't have to get the condo ready for the market wasn't a problem anymore. The insurance company was taking care of all the repairs, replacing the floors, fixing the walls, and painting. All of my furniture was out, and I was fine at Barron's place. My son and I planned the next phase to move the extra furniture out of his apartment. He was a big help and rented a U-Haul truck, and he drove the bulk of the furniture to my two sisters down south. One sister recently bought the house, and my older sister lived with her. They were trying to figure out how they would furnish the place, and they got a gift from me. Some of the pieces stayed at my son's place, and I gave the rest to my oldest sister who lived nearby.

I was back at work, feeling a sense of accomplishment but experiencing a sense of great loss and sadness nonetheless. I couldn't believe I would never sleep at my place again. Little did I know, when I left just before Christmas to spend the holidays with Barron, that that would be my final night living at home in my own place.

Now I was back to work, trying to make sure I was on top of things because I was planning a major event coming right up in March. Yes, I was in the thick of things, coordinating that event. Our company had been downsizing due to budget constraints. They had been laying off people for nearly a year now. But I felt safe and secure because of my role there. I was one of the people that others called with news about who was not there anymore.

Anyway, I was at my desk, and my supervisor asked me to join him in the conference room. I knew it was serious when I saw the human resources representative sitting at the end of the table. I was given an envelope package and told I was being riffed. This happened on January 30. I kept a straight face and didn't react. I felt like I had an out-of-body experience. It was like I listened and looked at my boss from a different dimension. When I returned from that moment, I glanced at him. I watched his mouth moving, looked at the human resources representative, and then back at him. I thought, *Oh Lord, how much more can I take?*

After more than fifteen years of dedicated service with this employer, I was told to pack up and leave the building in fifteen minutes. Dejected, hurt, and in shock, I smiled and calmly went to my office and collected my things. Apparently I was a bit too slow because I was asked to speed it up. I couldn't feel anything. I got along well with my supervisor, and he escorted me out to my car, which was much better than uniformed officers escorting me out. Life for me would never be the same.

It felt as if I floated to my car and hovered there until I could feel my body again. I don't know where my spirit went, but when I returned and could feel again, I drove home to Barron's place. I immediately told him what happened. He was calm. We talked. He listened and was very supportive.

Now, on top of the disaster with my condo that I was still coordinating, I was among the unemployed and must find another job. I knew for a fact that, deep down inside, I could never, ever go back to that employer after this shock of a lifetime. I thought, *Oh my goodness, I can't believe that I don't have a job.*

I cried because I couldn't believe it happened to me. It was very embarrassing and crushing. I knew I had to fight back because I had too much left to do and much more to offer. I had to hold it together and get through everything that was happening. I had to rely on the fact that things always worked out for me and it was for the best. This is a time in my life I'll always remember.

I had to get away, and I visited with my best friend, JacQui, in Northern California. We had a blast! I needed that. While away, I saw things more clearly and began to sincerely count my blessings and appreciate each of them. I was feeling better because the shock of the flood had worn off. I accepted my riff. I no longer had to worry about getting my condo ready for the market. I was really grateful that all the work being done to get my unit back in top shape was at no cost to me. I no longer had to worry about the floors, replacing carpet, moving furniture, or figuring out where my son or I would live in the interim.

I think back on my life that day in September 2013, when I knew it was time to make a change in my life and the angels gave me a plan. The only thing missing was a well-thought-out plan for me. So I prayed and surrendered my needs to God. Yes, I listened to my inner voice as it was guiding me along a different path long before the flood. It was good to urge my son to get his own place, and he listened. I was still figuring out where I'd live, and all that worked out too. God answered my prayer.

I didn't realize it when it happened, but I was in the midst of a miracle. They say that God answers your prayer and that it may not come the way you expect, but your prayer will be answered, if you only trust and believe. Oh, how happy I was when I realized all this. I was listening to my angels all along and didn't realize it. Something shifted inside of me when I was riffed. It took losing everything for me to let go of my life in that Excel spreadsheet. All that planning and monitoring went down the drain. I put down my laptop, opened my eyes, held my head high, and began to enjoy the present. Now to find that job!

I came home after my visit with JacQui a couple days right after Valentine's Day and immediately started looking for work. In my mind, I was starting to feel sure that things would work out. I bought a new laptop, a color printer, résumé paper, envelopes, and postage. My oldest sister helped by updating my résumé along with a fresh, new look. Lord knows I used it enough changing jobs at my previous employer.

I completed a job campaign the old-fashioned way by mailing cover letters with résumés, and I applied for jobs the modern way by completing the tedious online applications. I was hoping to find work in the federal government this time around. Still aloof about what was best for me, I applied for many local positions where the space would be in an office, and it finally hit me. I could apply anywhere in the United States and in other countries. That thought alone made the search much more interesting. Even if I did land a position and worked in an office, I could be in another state or country.

Now my focus was anywhere but the immediate area. My

new job could take me away, and I'd see more of the world. I applied and applied and applied. Nothing. No response. One day, I did get a response and had a telephone interview from a potential employer much farther up north on the East Coast. It turns out that I was overqualified for the job, but they encouraged me to continue looking for work at their organization. I did. Still nothing.

A close friend of mine invited me to go with her to Virginia Beach that April. She knew I needed a break.

I said, "Yes, I'll go!"

She drove, and we had a very nice time. I got up each morning and did my five-mile walk-jog routine while falling in love with *Neptune*, sculpted by Paul DiPasquale. That huge statue is strategically positioned along the boardwalk, and Neptune's image is well in command of the entire boardwalk. I was totally mesmerized as I passed him each morning. He literally made my day! I still have a beach towel she gave to me as a gift that has a large image of Neptune. She understood just how much I loved the entire experience.

She and I would catch the beautiful sunrise and sunset, we enjoyed our meals together, and we had wonderful long and meaningful talks. It was nice just to be away from all the pressure of finding a job. It was especially nice to know that I had friends who cared and wanted to cheer me up in such loving ways during one of the worst years of my life.

And that day came when I received a call from someone at my previous employer, six months after being riffed. The job offer really surprised me, and it was for less pay. I never once considered going back to that place. I was still too hurt and angry. But it was the one department headed by the one man at that employer who could convince me to return. His great character precedes him.

I was hired to start the last Monday of July. I reluctantly and jubilantly accepted the job offer. I know that seems like an oxymoron, but that's how I felt, angry and happy at the same time about my return.

Once there, I was very grateful, relieved, humbled, and, unfortunately, very uncomfortable. More good news followed. Since I had been separated from this employer for less than one year, I maintained all my benefits and the maximum leave accrual and continued on with my retirement savings plans. That was great! My return to work after being riffed, I thought, was a gift from God. Everything works out just the way it should because there are no mistakes, only lessons. The universe knows when you're ready to move on to the next phase because of continuous progression. Once you've conquered a lesson, then you move on to the next. Lord knows I'll never forget my lesson in trusting what a man says the first time he says it.

In reflection, my life as I once knew it had abruptly changed. That was the beginning of my awakening. I knew it was time for me to do something different well before the flood. I knew I needed another job even before I was riffed. But I did nothing absolutely nothing to change my life or my current circumstance. I was complacent and simply too lazy to step outside of my comfort zone. Now, once again, I was not true to myself and went back to the known.

Desperation will make you do foolish things. I simply bargained for less, which was the easy way out, and got exactly what I bargained for. I needed to get back to work, and I took the one and only job offer that came my way. There I was again, still learning that same lesson. Life would not and could not ever feel the same at work again. The air, trees, sidewalks, and colleagues all seemed different somehow. I felt hollow yet determined inside to keep it all together. I was simply going through the motions of life after a devastating yet freeing waterloo.

Chapter 3

Brokenhearted

From Rain to Sunshine

T he universe finds ways to send the same message until you get it. When that lesson is learned, you move on into the next phase of your life. I absolutely hated my new job and title. I had to keep my head held high because I needed the work and benefits. I hated everything about being back there. I detested my office, and I loathed that I had returned. I did not like the fact that I knew I had let myself down. I even hated that I hated being there.

I found out that one of my coworkers was riffed the same day that I was and we worked in the same department. We were the only two people riffed who were allowed to return to that employer. Her office was steps away and across from mine. We were acquainted with each other beforehand from special company projects in our roles, but didn't really know each other very well. My parking space was a bit down the road from the office, and she drove me to my car each evening that she could.

I love her for that because she went out of her way just for me. I wasn't used to that at all. Someone was helping me at work. We'd share our feelings about returning to the same employer, the same one who had let us both down and let us go like we were chopped liver. We discussed our pain and our continued disbelief that it happened at all. We became our own group therapy. We became great friends, and she gave me a new nickname, Spunky, because I used to take speed walk breaks at work for stress relief.

She'd say, "There goes Spunky!" when I left because I was already in my walking stride when I stepped past her office.

I asked her to join me, but she declined and politely reminded me that she drove everywhere to avoid walking and took the elevator to avoid the stairs.

Being riffed is like someone who took away your love, devotion, and sense of peace in less than a minute. You're caught off guard because everything that you thought you were at work, including your importance there, has been suddenly snatched away. The terrible feeling inside is emotionally draining and causes much distress.

One minute, you're living your-happy-go-lucky life, and the next, life will never, ever be the same. Everything looks different because you see the entire world differently. You feel different inside and out. That one negative act of being riffed tears you apart inside. You're left feeling stripped of all pride and dignity once felt on the job. You feel less than, ashamed, embarrassed, angry, dejected, and very hurt.

So yes, I betrayed myself by returning to the employer that took complete advantage of me and heightened all those negative emotions inside. I couldn't go on with such a negative attitude at work. It was wearing me down living in the fog. Apparently I still had that same lesson to complete. It was time to make a major change in my life. I was close, but not quite there.

I reached deep within and again thought of Dr. Wayne Dyer. "If you change the way you look at things, the things you look at change."

Seeing life now from a different perspective, I was very thankful to have a job, yet remained conflicted by my return. I was experiencing a tug-of-war inside, and it was physically draining, right along with an unhealthy mind-set. Many people back then were being let go from various large organizations, and the news of being riffed in waves was reported across the country. I found reasons to like my office and hate it at the same time. My office was right beside a dungeon.

So, you see, my Wayne Dyer perspective didn't last very long. The stench in that dungeon would seep into my office through the ceiling. And since I had the nerve to accept an office located in the basement, of all places, in an old building, I was begging for trouble. I already knew from when I was a young girl that I hated basements.

Coworkers would stop by and ask, "What's that smell?"

In my mind, I could see myself picking up a book and

throwing it at them for asking such an asinine question. I thought, *I don't control the damned air!*

That question angered and annoyed me to my bone marrow. I was extremely embarrassed by the smell and hated smelling it too. I take great pride in my surroundings and my atmosphere. I've been teased many times about being like Monk, a brilliant, fictional San Francisco detective with obsessive-compulsive disorder coupled with a fear of germs.

Anyway, I did the one thing I could do. I simply controlled my reaction. I'd compose myself to say, "Yeah, I know it's bad. It's coming from the dungeon beside my office."

Then they'd ask, "How can you take it every day?"

Well, you know how I feel about the first question, so imagine how I feel about this one.

I'd always heard about the dungeon but hadn't actually seen it. One day, I saw cleaning staff go into the dungeon to add water in a bucket for mopping the floor. I took a good look inside and saw just how old and ugly it was. The walls looked creepy, unfinished, and rusted. There was a big hole in the floor that led to only God knows where.

Born with a vivid imagination, I thought of all types of things living down there, like big alley rats, cockroaches, spiders, and, well, you get the picture. The lighting in the dungeon was very dim, gloomy, dingy, and uninviting, and on top of that, it was also the steam room. The humidity coupled with the old age, open floor, and decay of that room caused a stench like none other. I immediately thought to myself, *This is bad. It's not working for me.*

There was no way I could continue working here, knowing that my office was right beside that funky dungeon. I began to feel sick inside and out. I had a constant headache for weeks at a time, and my energy level was very low. I would get to work, see one or two dead cockroaches or spiders on my office floor, and get pissed off. The air-conditioner would malfunction nearly every week in the summertime. When that happened, we'd leave the side door open just to get the air circulating in the place.

Then one day, in came a squirrel! We all hopped on chairs and screamed. The poor little squirrel was also afraid and started screaming too!

I said to myself, "That's it for me. I've had it!"

That day was when I knew I had to leave. I didn't know when exactly, but I was mentally out the door. It didn't matter what I'd do next because the flip side of my job was the cause of my declining health, depression, and inner pain. I know. I know. You must recognize where you are today in life and really be thankful. I was thankful, and I did recognize my blessings. But I also knew that coming back to this employer had run its course, and it wouldn't be long before I made my next move.

In the meantime, I ordered an air dehumidifier and an air purifier for my office. It felt so much better. I would dump at least two gallons of water collected each day from the dehumidifier. I was extremely happy to feel environmental comfort. The purifier cleaned up the humidity and the odor. My office smelled and felt a whole lot better.

But by now, it was too little too late. Ticktock. Ticktock.

It was just a matter of time before I submitted my letter of resignation. I didn't have a plan yet, but I could feel it coming on strong. So I made a plan for what I could do today, draft my letter of resignation, which was a motivator for me. When I became frustrated at work, I'd go to my draft resignation letter and then read it and tweak it until I was satisfied. That was my little secret shared with no one.

In December 2014, my condo was still for sale nearly one full year later, and I was hoping a buyer would bite soon. I never slept there one night this entire year because, by the time Barron and I returned from California, I was still on leave for the holidays and was at his place when my son called with the news about the flood. I did get an offer for the condo back in August of that year, but the deal fell through. The prospective buyer vanished and would not return calls.

That experience was very unsettling because it felt like I was running out of time selling my condo. We immediately put it back on the market that August. I was hoping and praying that I could sell before New Year's. I had been paying all those bills by taking funds from my company retirement savings account. Yes, I know that wasn't the smartest thing to do, but it was the only thing to do to help myself in this situation. That riff caused a great wrinkle in my life, and I stopped living through my spreadsheets. My spreadsheets represented a period that the riff completely destroyed.

I was still in the midst of cleaning up the damage. That was such a rude awakening. At any rate, I didn't want to start 2015 with a mortgage. The day that the condo was back on the market, I prayed one last time and asked God for help like never before. I let it go and surrendered that entire situation to Him.

There were plenty of lookers and appointments, and one day out of the blue, the week before Thanksgiving, I got a call from my real estate agent with an offer. Yay! We negotiated and started the paperwork. The closing was scheduled on December 31, 2014. What a true blessing! I sold my condo at 11:00 a.m. on New Year's Eve! I was so happy to make that appointment. I couldn't wait to leave that meeting, knowing that this huge financial burden would finally be off my shoulders. I wasn't underwater, but I had to use more funds from my retirement savings to come up with my portion at the closing. After paying the mortgage and a few bills kept in place so the real estate agent could show my unit that entire year, I just wanted that situation to be over. I was finally done. I was free!

My niece was born on my birthday, and she is just like me when it comes to a job. She was restless and ready to leave the East Coast due to high housing costs. She and her husband wanted to move out of their suburban apartment into a house so their little girl could play in her own backyard and attend a great school. Housing alone kept them from that dream while living on the East Coast.

My niece started searching for different states to live in. You know that piqued my interest. She narrowed it down and selected Arizona. Her husband was totally against moving there and simply was not open to that notion. They took a trip to visit, and since he was closed-minded at the time, he was not impressed. They came back from that visit, and she kept searching for places to live in Arizona. She never gave up.

Eventually her husband decided to give it another try. He lined up three job interviews and flew out late May or early June 2015 and gained a newfound perspective about living in Arizona. He had a job offer before leaving the state. They had about one month to pack up everything and relocate. I was very happy for them, but it was like a smack in the face because I already knew that I had to make a major change in my life very soon too.

By the end of May 2015, I felt sick and weak. I hated going to work because I truly felt like my energy was completely zapped. I was tapped out. I lost a lot of hair on the top of my head. It fell out in patches. It had been close to a year, and I felt I betrayed myself by returning to work for the employer who stripped me of pride and dignity. I was depressed. I needed a way out of that place and fast.

In the meantime and while still holding down that job, I'd search for places to live in the United States just to boost my spirit enough to actually work that day and to show up for work the next. Arizona was looking pretty good. I didn't want my niece to think I was following her out there. Plus my son and I discussed finding a place to make my home, like some place in New England. I searched and searched, but nothing on the East Coast worked. My body and bones were reacting to the cold weather each winter, so I had to select a place where it's warm all year-round. Florida was out because of the summer weather patterns with hurricanes. I didn't want to worry about losing everything in another flood ever again.

I searched in the central United States and then Nevada, Hawaii, Oregon, and Washington, but there was absolutely no place that resonated with me. I applied for jobs in all those states too, and if I had landed a job in any one of them, I would have relocated there. Now I was only looking at the West Coast. I once lived in Northern and Southern California, so I didn't want to move backward. Not to mention that everything is too expensive in both locations. So I finally thought that Arizona was looking even better.

In June 2015, I had a series of doctor appointments. It turned out that my hair loss was not cancerous. Yay! I was depressed, but not clinically. My primary care physician agreed that I needed to make a change in my life because it was affecting my health. I had way too much stress. I was out on sick leave for a month, from the last week of May through the first three weeks in June.

Now that was over, and here I was, back at that damned job again, working for an employer who hurt me very deeply. And now my body was showing physical evidence that it was time to go. God and the angels knew that my return to that employer was important for me to get enough of that place and to never get comfortable there or anywhere else on the East Coast ever again. Did the angels send more signs or hints through others that I ignored? Was I that blind to the fact that my life was changing and everything that I was going through was part of the process? Why was my world still falling apart? Did the angels need to shout, "Get out of there!" from a megaphone? And did those words need to be written on the walls of my office?

I know now that I was not paying attention to all the clues from my angels. And I realized that I would repeat this lesson again and again until the universe knew I learned it inside and out. My lesson was to always be true to myself.

Barron showed compassion and support throughout my predicament. He didn't like seeing me so low in spirit, plus sickly. I'm usually very spunky and full of life. It's hard to keep pretending that everything is all right all day every day when it's not. I finally had to let go when I came home.

He understood and said, "Go ahead and plan that trip to Paris."

I said, "Really?"

That was music to my ears! Those words alone instantly helped me feel better. I was so excited about getting away to see the world. I finally had something to look forward to. It gave me something to do that was fun and something else to plan since my spreadsheets were practically useless.

All my life, I had wanted to visit Paris and London. Ever since I was a little girl, I fell in love with the old storybook, *Madeline,* because that cute little story took place in Paris at a Catholic boarding school. The twelve little girls wore uniforms with hats, and Madeline had such a zany imagination, willing to take risks. When I read those stories, I became Madeline in my mind. For that moment, I was happy planning our vacation to Europe, scheduled for the fall. The little girl inside of me was awake and very happy!

The big day came for my niece and her family to relocate. It was June 2015, and there were lots of family and friends at the airport to see them off. They too had lots of family support and lifelong friends that they'd miss. I walked with them to check their luggage curbside. My heart was getting heavier and heavier by the minute. I walked with them as far as I could go. My little four-year-old grandniece started crying when she realized that I was not going away with them.

My throat tightened, and my eyes filled with water. I hated seeing my niece born on my birthday, her daughter, and her husband look so sad. They were doing what they needed to do for their future. It was painful watching that moment unfold. They were strong and kept marching on, but their body language told another story. That was a very sad day for everyone at the airport.

There was something special about Arizona right from the start. Now that I had family there, I'd love to see them again and become part of their lives. Then I thought, *Would this move really benefit me?*

I started searching online for options of places to live and costs. Everything seemed so reasonable. Plus, the weather was just what I needed, lots of warmth and heat. I spoke with my primary care physician, and she agreed that Arizona would be a great place for me to live and regroup. I found the perfect apartment in downtown that really caught my eye. I thought, *If I ever move to Arizona, this is where I want to live!*

I would look at the floor plans almost every day and the surrounding area all the time. I fell in love with that high-rise apartment. And I was busy making plans for our vacation to Europe while thinking more and more about moving to Arizona. Life was looking up, and I was feeling better than I had in a very long time.

In September 2015, I had been working on our personal itinerary for the entire European vacation. I put together a very nice brochure with pictures of all the planned activities, including the dates and times of our adventures. I worked hard on that trip, and everything came together nicely. While wrapping up that trip, I decided to schedule another, my first trip to Arizona. Yes, I bought my round-trip ticket in September for my Christmas holiday in Arizona.

Deep down inside, I already knew the trip was really my chance to see and feel where I'd be moving to. Yes, I had my reasons, but I wasn't comfortable sharing my thoughts about moving with anyone. I still had things to do for my first-time visit to Europe. Barron had already seen Paris years before as part of his job, so I had to make sure I included places he hadn't been.

It was finally mid-October, and we were all packed and ready to go. When our limo arrived to take us to the airport, Barron's excitement caused him to miss the step at the front door, and he fell down on top of his luggage. He wasn't hurt at all, but he was quite embarrassed. We were finally about to board the plane.

The next thing I knew, we were landing at Charles de Gaulle Airport in France. I was too excited and ready to see Paris. I was living a dream. We were there for ten days. I was so amazed and captivated by the enormity of the Eiffel Tower.

It was great to get up each morning and jog through the park and beneath the Eiffel Tower. I couldn't get enough of that. We had dinner reservations on the top level of the Eiffel Tower too. We met the chef, took photos in a very clean, beautiful kitchen, and got an autographed menu, all after our six-course meal.

Another evening was spent at the Moulin Rouge. Such a great show, delicious food, and great service. I coordinated something special for Barron because he is a huge World War II buff. So we went on a Normandy battlefields and beaches day trip to see where so many American soldiers lost their lives fighting for our country in World War II.

Later in the week, we had an overnight trip to London, which was truly amazing. It was only about a two-hour train ride from Paris. We walked across the Westminster Bridge to get up close to Big Ben. Everything looked fantastic. When we first arrived, I loved seeing banners of US football teams hanging prominently across many of the streets. I didn't realize that Europeans were that interested in American football.

After our brief tour, we had a nice dinner there at one of Gordon Ramsay's restaurants. What can I say? The food was delicious! The next day, we were back in Paris early that afternoon. London was really great, but now I know that excursion should have been a separate trip all together. London is so beautiful, and we didn't have time to explore.

Back in Paris, our vacation was coming to an end, and I was feeling sad about leaving. Usually I'm ready to get back home after about the third night of any vacation. But over there, I felt a deep connection and honestly did not want to leave. I could have stayed and lived there happily ever after.

We were back in Maryland, and regardless of my European bliss, it's always a wonderful feeling getting back home to all your stuff. But for me, my mind was elsewhere, Arizona, and the apartment I found. I couldn't stop thinking about the place. I had already made plans to spend Christmas there. Now it was time to plan a trip to see family down south for Thanksgiving. Yes, that's how I like it—travel here and travel there. I'd just left Europe, and now I had plans to take the train to be with family for Thanksgiving and then off to Arizona for Christmas. Oh, how I love this!

Thanksgiving was great because it's always very healing to be among close family and friends. I always love reconnecting with my brothers and sisters, not to mention eating my portion of a great feast. During Thanksgiving holiday, I sat there alone one morning at the table, looking out through the patio doors at the beautiful green trees framed by such a big blue sky. That was the moment when I actually decided to move to Arizona, sight unseen. Something about the place beckoned me.

I thought about it all the time and began my job search there. The thought of Arizona was of great comfort and a positive feeling in my gut. I finally accepted the fact that my life in spreadsheets was a thing of the past. I got chills thinking about that awful day when I was riffed. And then I snapped out of it and thought about my new life over there in Arizona.

I was back to work. Nothing new was happening except for the fact that I knew something they didn't. I would retire at the end of June 2016 and relocate. Nobody knew that for a while but me. I wanted to keep that close to my heart and relish in that thought.

Christmas 2015 would be extra special this year because it would be a snapshot of my new life. I felt it as soon as I got off the plane at Sky Harbor Airport and as I walked through the airport to the baggage claim area. It was what I already knew would greet me. It was something hard to put into words. It was spirit.

I loved seeing my niece, her husband, and their little daughter that I was truly in love with. It felt right, like I knew it would. I couldn't stop smiling. You know that wonderfully warm feeling you get when things are unfolding as planned? Let me tell you. It's such an indescribable feeling of pure joy. That's what I felt, pure joy.

My oldest sister came out too that Christmas. She was ready to see her daughter and granddaughter. My niece took me to see the apartment I fell in love with online. It hit me like a ton of bricks when I looked up and saw it.

I said, "Oh my goodness, this is it! I will live there soon."

I enjoyed my visit to Arizona and was very sad to leave. I could hardly wait to return. The next time, it would be for good.

Back home, it was a few days before New Year's. I told Barron about my decision to relocate. He was surprised, to say the least, because he mentioned in a previous conversation that I could stay with him indefinitely. He always had my back. I had his too, but it wasn't about being there for each other. It was more about new beginnings for me. It was finally time for me to find my passion and myself.

Although he was very sad to know I'd be moving across the country and leaving him and the East Coast for good, he supported my decision. Feeling freer than ever before, I knew these were life-changing decisions. My entire life on the East Coast was completely dismantled, and it was up to me to rebuild a whole new life for myself. I also knew that I was on the right path because it felt right. You know it's right when you make a decision without consulting anyone and when your body feels calm and peaceful simply by the thought of easing into a new life. I was feeling a new sense of independence, like the Diana Ross song, "It's My Turn."

Barron and I celebrated New Year's together. It was 2016. Who knew back in June, when I was planning our trip to Europe in the fall, that in December I'd share the news about retiring from my job and relocating to Arizona? When you're on the right track, things tend to unfold fairly rapidly. We talked about going to Paris for many years and never made real plans until we finally did.

God always assists us in His way. He chose the perfect time that was in season with all of my life-changing decisions. After our time abroad, I returned stronger and ready to handle my business. Who knew that our European vacation would be the trip of a lifetime for us and our final trip together? Although Arizona was on the horizon, I'll always remember our time together in Europe for as long as I live.

It was still January, and moving plans were underway. I was working my timeline, which included benchmark dates for many things, like going through clothes and boxing them for Goodwill donations, packaging boxes for shipments to my niece, selecting a date to purchase my one-way airline ticket, and finally scheduling a company to transport my old car from here to Arizona. That was a lot, especially while at the same time holding down my job.

On one hand, I was happy and inspired about my plan for a fresh start, but on the other hand, I felt sad about leaving Barron, who had been my rock for so many years. Most of all, I felt sad about leaving my son again. Yes, my son was an adult now, doing quite well in his life, but he would forever be my baby boy. I had to get over all of that to stay focused. Yes, that meant I had a reason to create new spreadsheets just to keep myself on track with all the things I needed to do for a smooth transition into my new life.

Back at work, I was bored and frustrated because I was anxious and ready to go. I had a feeling that I would finally find myself, understand who I really was, and come to grips with all the decisions leading up to this point. On top of that, I knew it was only a matter of time for me to learn something new and very special about myself.

But back to reality, work became almost unbearable: the dungeon beside my office, dumping water from the dehumidifier, and the noise from that machine and the air purifier. Plus I was holding down a lackluster job. I just didn't want to be there. It was hard to continue working on a job when you have a made-up mind to leave. That is a place of mental turmoil because of the constant daily struggle with getting the job done and finding the inspiration to do it.

Stress found a way to get me out of that turmoil sooner rather than later. Things seemed worse than what they were because I allowed negative power and energy to take over my thoughts, and that negativity grew more each day. My health helped me with my final decision to move and to change the way I was thinking. It was past time for me to feel a sense of accomplishment. I had a plan, and it was working. How about that? I could hardly wait to speak to the human resources representative to discuss my retirement options and a suggested official retirement date.

And that day came when I submitted my letter of retirement. When I handed my boss the letter, he didn't want to read it because he knew what I was doing. He's such a nice man and well respected by so many people. But this was my day to celebrate completing a major task on my things-to-do list. I could finally see and feel the bright sunshine. Today's work was now peaceful compared to yesterday's frustration. Everything suddenly felt different. I felt lighter. Nature appeared more vibrant than ever before. I was calm and at peace with myself because I fell in love with me. Now my wants and needs were first!

That had been a very long time coming. I felt a sense of confidence like never before. I said no to laborious projects instead of saying yes because it was right for someone else. I began to feel that my needs, wants, and desires really were important instead of always pleasing someone else. I started treating myself with love, grace, and tenderness. I no longer felt conquered by the words of others.

So I made more time for myself by improving my health and started walking again. I lost weight and felt like a million bucks. Then I accepted this notion, *How could I ever expect someone else to love me if I didn't love myself or put myself first?* It took a while to get to know myself and reconnect with all of me. A perfectionist by nature, I am still working on not being so hard on myself when plans get off track. There's nothing like an awakened spirit who leads and guides you to all the wonderful things you used to love, only to find out that you still love many of those things and more. My inner child loves the book and life of *Madeline*, but now through our eyes—the eyes between myself and the little girl within—we love each moment together just as we are.

In reflection, Barron loved listening to music on Sundays, and we'd sit together for hours listening to all kinds of great music on his top-of-the-line stereo equipment. I don't think he realized just how much I resonated with one of Adele's old songs from her debut album *19*, "Chasing Pavements."

The lyrics mirrored how I felt for so many years of our relationship. I mentioned wanting more once or twice, but he wouldn't budge. Looking back, sometimes I wondered how we stayed together for all those years. Then I'd resolve that our close friendship kept us together as companions, but there was always something missing, passion. I finally made the decision to go in a different direction and live a new life.

Now as I retrain my brain to think more positively, I'm a happier person because of it. Thoughts are things. Life really does get better if you trust and believe, all echoed by determined action instead of wallowing in self-pity and living brokenhearted.

Chapter 4

Reflections

Silhouettes at a Distance

"There has to be more to life than this." That thought crossed my mind each day and with every beat of my heart. Yes, that feeling haunted me all the time, and I thought there was nothing I could do about it. It felt as though I was watching myself from the sideline while seeing my whole life tick away. Ticktock. Ticktock.

Now whenever I feel unappreciated or unfulfilled, I think more about the opposite and keep moving on. But why did I have that feeling in the first place? What I've learned from my past experiences is that, in order to move forward, I had to face my past and deal with it head-on by acknowledging and accepting each and every aspect. Life is like a million-plus-piece puzzle. You must find each tiny piece of you to fill those moments of your life, bringing you closer to a finished puzzle.

Silhouettes at a distance are those pieces of my life that

I never understood, sections pushed aside and clueless as to where they'd fit in. We all know that a puzzle is never complete while we're here on earth because the final piece represents the day we return to spirit. I had to learn to face my truth and accept it for what it is so that portion of my life's puzzle is finally put together. Then and only then will you move on to the next section.

One of the hardest sections of my life's puzzle was about forgiveness. We all can forgive someone for mistreating us, but do we really? If you honestly forgive someone, then you would treat him or her as you did before that something happened. Truth is, we tend to place the person and the questionable or hurtful act in a file deep in our minds where the incident is never forgotten, but it is replayed over and over again in our minds and each time we see the individual. So we believe we've forgiven that person, and we sincerely believe we have.

But from that point on, we keep this person at a safe distance and go on with our lives. Are you treating the individual as you did before the incident? Did you really forgive him or her? Does this person still cause pain and cognitive dissonance by the mere thought of the act that led to the crumbling of the relationship in the first place?

As humans, we generally hold on to those negative moments, and then we keep those who hurt us at a comfortable distance. I know it depends on the situation, but if we stop for a moment and try to understand what the real problem might be, we may see that silhouette of a person we never knew existed. Then we might find more pieces to the puzzle and place them in the area of forgiveness.

Try not to get stuck on one section, especially if certain pieces look too difficult to manage right now. That means you've come face-to-face with an issue, and only time can help with answers to your many questions or heal that particular deep hurt inside. Eventually, each section of the puzzle will make even more sense, and you'll find yourself moving right along by placing the next piece in the next section. At the same time, your life is shifting for the best.

Reflections of the past can be unpleasant. I think back to 1965, when my family first moved from the South to the North. For three weeks, we lived in an old, ugly, dingy, smelly basement apartment that was simply disgusting. We had a house to move into, but it wasn't quite ready. For some reason, Dad couldn't wait to move. We left the South in a hurry. He knew the house wasn't ready, so he did the best he could in finding shelter for his family. He believed that a short stay in that, sight unseen, pit from hell would be okay. Mom cleaned up the place nicely, but for me, I'll never forget the initial sight and smell.

I remember getting away in my mind while watching Superman on our little black-and-white television. Aluminum foil was at the top of the antenna so we could receive the channel. I loved seeing Superman get caught and then get away!

If there were nothing to watch on television, I'd go outside and walk along the round cement base of the fence by our dwelling. The fence ended in a V shape right at the corner of that block. I'd only walk to the end of the fence because, even then, I wasn't too trusting of strangers. Thinking about this time in my life is painful, not only because of where we were living, but because I have absolutely no memory of my two younger brothers being there with us at that awful place. Now that I think about it, I don't recall my older siblings were there too. I was five years old, old enough to remember, but I don't.

The house was finally ready, and we moved out of that basement. Hallelujah! The difference was like night and day. Really! I loved this row house but hated the basement. Yet I even played in the basement sometimes with cousins and friends who lived nearby.

Yes, I do remember my two younger brothers and all of my siblings at this location. And even today, I really dislike basements of all kinds. I don't care how beautiful it is. If I must spend time in a basement, then it must have sunlight shining through regular-sized windows and a door that can actually open and welcome you to a beautiful outdoor arrangement of some kind. So when you're actually sitting there, it doesn't feel like you're in the basement.

When I think about my life back then, living with my parents, five brothers, and three older sisters, life was really something special, sacred, and very beautiful. I do regret that I was too young then to fully appreciate how blessed I was, living each day with all my immediate family.

As we all know, the older you get, the years seem to pass by pretty fast. When I think back on prom night, it was for someone else's high school graduating class of 1977 and a night I'll never forget. That night, my close friend and former next-door neighbor to our first real house up north was in that graduating class. She was so excited to go to her prom. She and her boyfriend had it all planned out.

She called me the night of the prom to see if I would go with her neighbor who was stood up. I sort of knew him too from years back. He was a nice guy, and I felt sorry for him. Luckily I already had something to wear. I met her at her house, and we all went together.

The neighbor and I said we'd walk in together, and that was it. It worked. He had fun, and so did I. I don't remember how he got home, but he didn't ride back with us. I was glad to help create a happy moment in his life, at least at the beginning of his prom night.

That following year, I didn't go to my own prom. I had no desire because I went to three different high schools during my senior year, one back east, one in Northern California, and the last at a different location back east. My high school pictures are from my first high school. I have nothing to show from the second high school on the West Coast, and I graduated from the third high school back east. I loved all of that movement, and in the end, I was happy to finally graduate high school.

Much to my surprise, I ended up loving my last high school because I became a member of the choir. We had a great group of singers. During my graduating year, 1978, we entered the adjudication competition, and we won first place with a fifty-voice choir by singing our butts off! We were so afraid the other school's choir with 250 voices would win. They came in second place. That was a great day and a moment I will never forget.

On graduation day, choir members were asked to come forward to sing as part of the graduation program. I proudly got up from my seat to join the choir. We performed well. I walked back and forth a couple times with other choir members to sing. I thought that only JacQui was at my high school graduation because she was with me as I drove myself in my sister's Ford Fairmont.

A few days before, when I asked if anyone in the family would be there, everyone said he or she couldn't. Back then, our family participated in high school graduations and made sure they were there for the event because, in our immediate family, no one had continued on to college.

I remember my older brother's graduation with lots of family around. He graduated in 1976 from the first high school I went to as well as two of my older sisters. My brother and I attended that high school together just for a short while. I started high school during his senior year. I was so excited to go to his graduation with all my family because I could see how it would be for mine.

Much to my surprise when I came home, I found out that my parents made it to my graduation after all. I can't remember if anyone else showed up, but they were the most important ones there. I'm glad they made it. It sure would have been nice knowing they were there during the ceremony.

As far as prom night, I've never looked back with regret, thanks to that young man who was stood up. I went with him, saw what a prom was like, and knew that was enough for me. When I think about not going to my own prom, I could choose to be sad or feel sorry for myself. But that has never, ever been my feeling about prom night. I was simply not interested in going. Sure, there were moments I dreamed of going with the great football star back then from my first high school, but that was all it was, just a dream. That guy never knew I existed. I'm fine with it.

I loved attending those three different high schools my senior year. That alone was a challenge in adapting to different situations and meeting new people. I'm a stronger person today with great skills in adapting to most any situation because of it.

I realize now that my life is a body of work that is put together moment by moment in a well-crafted glass frame of thoughts, ideas, and beliefs. Every now and then, my picture falls from the wall to the ground, and the glass on the outside shatters. The picture is on the ground, with a hole or two, and is picked up and placed in another glass frame, only to fall to the ground. And the glass shatters once again. Why? Because the picture—symbolic of my life—was not hung properly.

It took a while before I finally understood that I would continue to repeat lessons from the past if I failed to open my eyes and see what was actually happening. If I never look at the big picture, I will only see a smaller picture, as it is only part of the overall picture. That smaller version can lead to trouble because, when you focus only on your life, the big picture is lost. That means I had to learn to focus on the greater good for everyone in everything and in all aspects of my life. With that notion, I've learned to love myself so I am able to love others without condition. I've learned to place myself on solid ground in a shatterproof frame of thoughts, ideas, and beliefs so I have time to heal.

All my pain from old cuts, bruises, and holes from broken heartedness finally had time to heal. When I've allowed myself all the precious time needed to reflect, understand, and accept myself and every moment lived, I've given myself permission to heal, and move on. The puzzle is coming together. As a result, I'm stronger and more focused. Best of all, I've learned to love myself in the process.

And that day came when I finally understood that I was getting what I gave from my dad. In my younger years, we never had a close relationship. Now I realize that I too played a part in that. Not only did he intimidate me by sometimes yelling with his big, booming voice, I know I must have given him good reason with some pretty mean looks and very bad body language too. We went tit for tat, and we were both wrong for that. I would stomp up the stairs as hard and loud as I could, trying to crack each step. Then I'd slam my bedroom door with all my might. I could hear him laughing because I had the nerve to do that.

He and my mom knew that not a single one of my siblings in the first family would ever even think about doing such a thing. Yet, here I was, around twelve or thirteen, ready and willing to get on his nerves and suffer the consequences. We received what we gave to each other, and it was not a lot of love. I forgave myself, my little girl, for being so angry, and I forgave my dad too for not showing love and attention, which led to negativity impacting both our lives well into our future.

My work life filled with office jobs and the men who played major roles in my character development were all lessons about my relationship with myself. None of the jobs resonated with me. No surprise there. None of the guys truly resonated with me. So why did I stay? I stayed for the challenge and the losing battle, out of survival, security, and companionship. I can apply Maslow's hierarchy of needs to my life's choices, and everything lies in level two.[2] There are five levels in all:

1. Physical: the need for air, food, water, rest, and health
2. Security: the need for safety, shelter, and stability
3. Social: the need for being loved, belonging, and inclusion
4. Ego: the need for self-esteem, power, recognition, and prestige
5. Self-actualization: the need for development and creativity.

Man! And here I was feeling like I was stuck on level two. It's nice to know when it's time to give up everything. I was not aligned with my higher self, and I knew it. I just didn't understand that I created this world for myself.

In reflection, we set the course of our lives with our thoughts, intentions, and actions. What we choose to focus on is what gets the attention, power, and energy through the law of

---

[2] https://www.psychologytoday.com/us/blog/hide-and-seek/201205/our-hierarchy-needs

attraction. I've learned that, if I choose to focus on what comes so natural for me, the negative, then that's just what I'll get. On one hand, it takes no effort to think that way.

On the other hand, it does take effort to develop the habit of thinking clearly, positively, and toward my future. I've learned to stay focused and to get back on track when I feel myself slipping off or back into negativity. I do look forward to the day when most of my thoughts are clear, positive, light, and easy. Then I will have garnered the skill to trust and believe that everything always works out for the best. That's positive power and energy. I cleverly chose this life, which includes all my creations seen in many reflections.

Chapter 5

I Surrender

How Can This Be?

I was working my plan to move to Arizona, and things were really coming together. Ah, what a relief. It's so amazing how life changes when you make a decision that's right for you. My life felt better. Things weren't as worrisome. I felt lighter and in a better mood. I had a brighter outlook on life. Why? Because it was the right thing to do and I could feel it deep down inside. I'd planned out everything to make this move happen, which included giving up most everything I had.

Remember, when my condo flooded, I gave away all my furniture. I moved back in with Barron and couldn't crowd his place with all my things. So life worked out such that I didn't need to. Now that I was there with him, I tried very hard to keep the things that I did move neatly stacked and out of sight as much as possible, while knowing that I couldn't take most of it when I relocated.

I set a schedule to go through all my clothes and stuff from January through April 2016. I gave myself an April deadline to coincide with my scheduled Goodwill pickup date. Each weekend, I went through my things, separated, boxed, and labeled clothing. I followed the guidelines of Goodwill for the pickup. That was not a fun task. I never knew that so many feelings go into giving up things. It's amazing how deeply attached to certain pieces that once had great meaning to your life could have such a great hold on you. There's a television show about hoarders, and I even began to understand them a bit more because of the difficulty I had in letting go of so many things at one time. It really is challenging. Yes, after I got into it, I soon realized that my life was different now. I made peace with many things given up, and I was finally moving on as I brought this chapter of my life to a close.

My weekends went on the same, focused on packing and shipping boxes to my niece in Arizona, six total, by sending two medium-sized boxes at a time each Saturday. At home, I began to see how my hard work was paying off and how all my things in Barron's home were clearing out. Once May rolled around, I made arrangements to have my car transported. I was really happy to get that done. The only thing left to do was buy my one-way airline ticket to Phoenix.

But before I did all that, I needed an in-depth self-check. *What's happening to me? Why am I feeling so compelled and deeply moved to relocate to Arizona?*

Yes, I loved my niece very much, and her daughter was like the light of my life. She and her husband moved to Arizona the previous year, and I missed the three of them dearly. But that wasn't the pull. Yes, I needed new surroundings. Yes, I wanted to move someplace with meaning, where I could find deep spiritual meaning, like the state of Arizona. The vortex and the sacred mountains of Sedona were calling me too.

That aside, I questioned my entire life. I didn't want to face my intuitive side, so I brushed it off quickly and wondered, *Why now?* I was in deep denial about my gifts. I knew I wanted much more out of life, but I didn't know where to begin. I only knew that my life was waiting for me elsewhere and I had to find it. I was simply afraid to explore my intuitive gifts because I was really scared of ghosts. I thought it would be something very odd, like in *Carrie* or *The Exorcist*. Those old films scared me so badly until I'd be afraid to do anything alone for months. I was so afraid until I simply had to stop watching scary movies period. I was already afraid of the dark as a child and sometimes now.

As a child, once I could separate the movie from reality, that really helped. That's why I believe that it's so important for parents not to allow kids to see horror films or scary television shows before their little minds understand what they're seeing. As an adult, I've learned that some of the horror films are based on real-life events. That didn't make matters any easier. In fact, that scared me even more, knowing how life can be so different or as portrayed in those scary movies.

I felt very vulnerable, knowing I had some kind of connection to something I did not understand. I was mentally paralyzed due to my vivid imagination, and the last thing I wanted to do was explore my natural gifts. It was simply too much to bear. I latched on to anything that gave me pause from exploring the unknown or the intuitive side. I remained frozen and incapable of moving forward with my natural intuitive gifts.

Day by day, it became easier to ignore the fact that I was different. I buried that notion so deep within until I totally forgot about it. I became average and lived a normal life. I was successfully unplugged. Even then, I felt a huge void inside. I knew there was more to life, but I simply wasn't ready to explore. It caused a great conflict of emotions that I couldn't seem to ignore or push away. I thought, *Ignoring my intuitive gifts is easy.*

I thought so at first, but as it turns out, I outsmarted myself and allowed human illness to set in, like hypertension. Things bothered me so much so at work until the whites of my eyes would turn red. I absolutely hated my job. I was so out of alignment with whom I really was and what I volunteered to do with this incarnation on earth. This misalignment affected every aspect of my life.

One day, I decided to do something about it. I started slow by reconnecting with nature. I found out that, if I lost weight, exercised, and ate better, my life would automatically be better because I'd see things from a different perspective. I needed that.

Gone are the days of playing the victim, of not being able to speak my truth at work or home, with friends, and simply everywhere. I was so out of balance. I could feel my life getting worse if I didn't stop and gain some control over what I allowed in my personal space.

Before I reconnected with nature, I asked, "Why me? Why was I born differently than all my siblings?"

I'm the seventh child of nine and blessed with gifts I thought I neither wanted nor understood. My mom said I was born with a veil over my face, a fact that my oldest sister shared with me. So again I asked, "Why me?"

After getting through this dark period in my life, things began to make a little sense. Nature truly helped me to reconnect. I'd go for long speed walks in the park filled with tall, beautiful oak trees. I loved every minute. I felt a strong connection with those big, beautiful oak trees, the grass, the running water from the creek, the family of deer, the birds, the beautiful flowers, and so on. I started to appreciate all the priceless gifts of nature in all my surroundings and found peace.

During morning walks, sometimes five miles per day before going to work, I felt great all day! I felt rejuvenated inside and very grateful to be alive. Everything seemed much brighter and happier to me. My thoughts also reflected my newfound spirit. Yes, I had finally found my spirit. But I knew there was much more waiting to be discovered. All these wonderful feelings inside from my reconnection with nature helped for a time until I became conflicted again with my entire life and my spirit. I wanted to be free. I wanted to travel and see the world. I knew, beyond the shadow of a doubt, that I was not cut out for a regular nine-to-five job, period.

God help me! Even as a child, I never, ever wanted to work

in an office. I wanted to be an artist, singer, actress, dancer, or writer. I wanted to do something related to the arts. But life has a way of making decisions for you ... if you do nothing. Well, I did nothing and got more of the same.

I had my son at the young age of twenty-one. I felt ashamed only because I was not married. It was in the early 1980s. Back then, society was pretty tough on single moms. Luckily for me, I'm from a large family, and my parents and sisters helped a lot. I can never repay them for the unconditional love shown to both my son and me way back then. I'm still surrounded by lots of loving family who love and care about the two of us dearly. Remember, my father was a minister, and my mom was an evangelist. My brothers, sisters, and I were preacher's kids!

I went away to California after high school and managed to return home with a child. That was big. In hindsight, it was for the best because my life would not be the same without him. I conformed to the norms of society. I found a good office job, but not in the arts, and stayed there until I physically and mentally could not take it another day.

I provided my son with everything I thought he needed and some of what he wanted. I did my very best to make up for the fact that his dad was never a part of his life. I carried that guilt ever since he was born. It was tough letting that one go. Now I understand and know myself better.

And that day came when I finally boarded the airplane, moving forward to a brand-new life that awaited me, full of unknowns. High up in the air, staring out the window while looking at the fluffy white clouds in the big blue sky, I saw the thinnest streak of light in my future. Something more was out there for me to know, to discover, and to experience. I had to find a way to get closer to that light.

Yes, I knew that included lots of change in myself in order to grow spiritually. This is the most challenging part. I had to make major life-changing decisions because, before today, I did nothing to get closer to the light. Now I know that choosing my life's path was always up to me.

In reflection, I knew that all of it, every aspect of my life, had to change. That was my elephant in the room. I started first by literally looking deep into my eyes in the mirror. I finally saw myself and didn't like my reflection. I looked okay on the outside, but inside, I felt like a bird with broken wings.

Yes, I was broken. I knew I wanted to fly but didn't know how. I knew there was much more out there in this big, beautiful world for me to see and explore, but I couldn't move. I was stuck, standing on the edge, and afraid to try to fly. All those thoughts crossed my mind as I stood there, really seeing myself in the mirror for the first time. I took a deep breath and exhaled. I accepted the fact that I needed to find myself. When the airplane landed in Arizona, I felt an immediate connection to my surroundings, I gave up my old life for a new one, and here I stood with open arms.

I finally found the courage to jump out of the nest to fly away. Yes, I surrender.

Part II

When we realize that God is always there with us, for us, nothing is unbearable. When we realize that our "waterloo" is the beginning of magnificence, then we finally accept who we are.

Chapter 6

Cocoon

Finding Myself Within

On June 26, 2016, I finally made it to Arizona. My departure from the East Coast and landing in Arizona had very special meaning to me. My dad had passed away on June 26 in 2011. I picked that date so I'd always remember when I started my new life.

My niece and her daughter greeted me at Sky Harbor Airport. Lord knows I was so happy to see them! The newness of it all was a bit overwhelming. On one hand, I was really glad to be here, and I knew I made the right decision. But on the other hand, I didn't like being this far away from my son, and it was hard to believe that I gave up everything. I gave up my entire life as I once knew it and my spreadsheets for a fresh start. I knew this wouldn't be easy, but I was determined to move on, and I remained open to all that would unfold.

At this time, my little grandniece was five years old. I

simply adore her. Just being in her presence brightens my day, and she gives me spiritual inspiration and strength. My niece's husband is a wonderful dad.

So I was out here with the three of them, living in their beautiful home. That within itself is very different for me because I'm very independent. I like having my own place and feeling in total control of my life. Now I was not. Yes, I could have set up moving into my own apartment, but I felt like being with family. I wanted to start out doing something that I wouldn't normally do and made peace with it.

I felt so free now. But it's hard to describe how I actually felt on the inside. Sometimes I thought back to my old life and wondered, *What took me so long to uproot myself for a more peaceful life?*

With time on my side, I planned to start looking for a job after Labor Day. I wanted to give myself a much-needed mental break while becoming acclimated to my new surroundings. So I'd get up every day and drive my little niece to school, come back home and rest, and watch a little TV. Then it was time to pick her up from school because she had half-days in kindergarten. I loved seeing the look on her little face when I picked her up and when she got home to see the snack I made for her on the counter.

When her parents came home, I'd hang around for a bit and soon make myself scarce so they'd feel some sense of normalcy now that I was living in their space. When I was upstairs in my room, I tried to make it as cozy as possible. It took a while to empty the boxes and fully unpack. This was an ongoing process for a while.

But in the interim, I found new doctors one morning while my little niece was at school. Some things in my life had to continue, even though I was in a new state. My health was the priority, and everything else simply fell into place.

It was July, and we were excited about the holiday. The Fourth was coming right up! We planned to spend time in the backyard by the pool, cook out on the grill, and just enjoy the day. Later, we'd go out and find a nice spot to see fireworks light up the sky. We did just that and had a ball. Wow! Things were beginning to feel really good.

Out of the blue, I started to feel like I was catching a cold or virus of some kind. I ignored it and kept moving. I continued with my routine of taking my little niece to school, picking her up, and enjoying the rest of the day. I began to feel worse day by day. It was hard to walk up and down the stairs, and it was difficult to get around in general. I sensed that my body was going through a change. I couldn't put my finger on it, but it was getting worse and worse by the hour.

It was hard shaking that feeling, so I went to the doctor on Thursday, July 7. I was given a prescription for antibiotics. For some reason, I felt that my new primary care physician wasn't as focused as she could have been. I immediately picked up my prescription and took the medicine, but it didn't help at all. So the next afternoon, I called my doctor's office to let them know that I felt really bad and was getting worse. I was told to keep taking the antibiotics and come in to see my doctor on that following Monday.

I couldn't believe my ears. I could hardly get around, and it was a chore to walk up and down the stairs. It was Friday, and they wanted me to keep feeling this way or worse until Monday. *Oh well*, I thought.

I was too tired, weak, and sick to fight to see my doctor that day. So I decided to wait until Monday. My energy level dropped drastically. It was like I was slowly dying. I couldn't figure out what it was or why I was having these worsening symptoms.

When my niece saw me barely making it downstairs that Saturday morning, she stopped doing everything and said, "I think you should go to urgent care." There are plenty of places like that in Arizona. She quickly changed her mind and said, "No, I'll take you to the emergency room, just in case you need to be admitted."

She was right. I was admitted moments after, registering with pneumonia. My oxygen level was 9 mmHg (millimeters of mercury; unit of pressure measurement), when normal is between 95 to 100. Also I had low potassium and low phosphate.

I don't remember the first night there in the hospital. That entire evening is a big blur because I was so out of it. It felt like I was in a cocoon, turning into a new being. Yet it's hard to find the right words to express how I felt, but I knew more was waiting for me.

I found it. I went to someplace else, a spiritual place, or the other side. I had a peaceful visit with my parents in the spirit world. I don't remember all of my visit, but I know I was there with the two of them. We sat together at what looked like a dark brown wooden table, and they talked while I listened.

I wanted to stay, but they sent me back because it wasn't my time to stay. They reminded me that I had much work to do. Even though I left for a nanosecond while hooked up to an IV and other machines, my life changed that night forever. When I awakened that Sunday morning, it was like I had a deeper connection with myself within. I shifted.

They also tested me for valley fever, and thank goodness, the test was negative. My niece visited, and on one of those times, she brought her daughter. I was so glad to see that little girl, and she was excited to see me too. She drew these girly, women figures on a whiteboard of her mom, her grandmother, and me. Her drawing was beautiful. I loved it, and so did all the nurses. I took a picture of her artwork with my iPhone because my niece, my little niece, and myself are on this journey together. We are the three amigos! Somehow I have an extremely deep spiritual connection with the two of them.

For three days and two nights, I was there in that hospital. By Monday morning, I couldn't wait to leave. That evening, July 11, I was finally released. I felt like a new person with lots of energy. I was given a second chance at life, and I wasn't gonna blow it for anyone or anything. I was so glad to see my niece pull up to take me home. That beautiful, shiny, black Cadillac sedan could not have looked any better! It felt like my stagecoach, and I was Cinderella, dressed and going to a ball. But the ball was really and truly my new life. I thought, *What if*

I decided to move into my own place upon arrival to Arizona? It's a good thing I decided to do something different and live with family out here. What if my niece hadn't taken me to the emergency room? Would I have made it to see Monday morning to see my doctor like the assistant said?

All I know is that I couldn't think for myself clearly, and I was slowly ticking away. I don't want to imagine what could have happened. My niece took action and saved my life. Yes, there is an undisputed connection between us.

Moving on, my spirit had been energized. And guess what? Just like America faced a tragedy in Pearl Harbor on December 7, 1941, we rose up and became the most powerful country in the world. Well, my niece and I are both born on Pearl Harbor Day, and we have many of the same personality traits. We are both rising up into our own power. She came to earth twelve years after me and selected the same family. I left the hospital feeling some kind of deep spiritual connection and thought, *I am awake.*

I came home to a clean, beautiful room. My niece and her little daughter worked so hard to make things nice for my return. I love them both so much! She knows how I love cleanliness and beauty. I appreciated everything they did for me. It really touched my heart. When I spoke with my oldest sister on the phone that day, she told me that my niece was afraid to go back to see me after I was admitted to the hospital because she thought I might die. What a thought! Because I believe I did for just a nanosecond.

Like me, my niece is highly intuitive. Her daughter is too.

So things turned back to normal soon. I was on a path to the unknown with no resistance. But each day, I knew I was getting closer and closer to why I am here.

In August 2016, I felt like it was time to figure out why I was in Arizona, why it beckoned me so. I made an appointment to have my first intuitive reading on Sunday, August 28. My niece found and recommended Terri Tucker for my first reading before I even moved to Arizona. She told me that Terri gave excellent psychic readings.

It's true. Terri helped me to think outside the box and to keep searching for why I'm here. She knew things that only someone intuitively gifted could ever know. I was so completely satisfied. Her reading helped me to know that I was at the very beginning of everything new and all of the major changes in my life were truly meant to be. That was a great day. I had never had a reading before, and I felt so positive and motivated when I left. And I wanted more.

Now it was the first week of September, just after Labor Day. It was time to seriously focus on finding a job. Oh, I had been looking for a job since I first came in late June, but not at a vigorous pace. Now I was led to plan a trip to Sedona for spiritual healing.

After having pneumonia, my new awakening, and my first reading, intuitive things just kept falling into place. I found someone in Sedona I thought I'd love, and I did. I drove up alone, my first time going any real distance alone in Arizona, and I enjoyed the entire experience. I had a wonderful tour up in the mountains, and I could feel the spirits there in the vortex, such a very spiritual place. I couldn't believe how majestic everything looked and the great feeling I felt inside. My spirit was happy. I found peace. I knew I was getting close to why I gave away all that I had and left loved ones for my new life in Arizona.

Back home from a long weekend in Sedona and still feeling the spiritual well-being, I knew I'd find a job soon. So looking for a job was my job after dropping off my little niece at school every day. But first I gave myself permission to be off that Monday because I needed that day to think about my life, to reflect, and to feel the newness of it all. That Tuesday, September 13, I was looking full-speed ahead. I had to keep telling myself, *You've been seriously looking for less than a month.*

I was getting frustrated because I had no bites and no interviews lined up. Nothing. It reminded me of the time when I was riffed and the only company who showed interest was the same company who had riffed me in the first place. Over here, everything was fresh and new, but there was no soft place to land as far as finding a job. I had no contacts out here, which felt very uncomfortable. Things did get better.

Thoughts are things, and thoughts are very powerful. I never realized that, by thinking my current situation with looking for work reminded me of the time when I was riffed, I was actually sending a message to the universe to do the same thing as before, to send another job my way that I really didn't want.

Sixteen days later, on September 29, I got an email asking

if I were still interested in a job I applied for my first day of job hunting after my trip to Sedona. I replied "Yes!" and we set up the appointment for my interview. It was so exciting! I finally had an interview. I drove to the place days ahead to become familiar with everything, where to park, and which building the office was located in. I couldn't afford to be late.

I parked, walked inside the building, took the elevator up to where the interview would take place, turned around, and left. I wanted to see and feel the place and all the surroundings. Oh yes, this was happening, and I knew the job was mine before the interview.

Before going to my car, I decided to take a good look around to see if I were near the apartment I fell in love with before I moved here. Lo and behold, I could see it, and it was in walking distance. I walked there to see it again up close. I loved it! I turned around and walked to my car and drove back home. I declared that I would live there and would walk to work.

On Monday, October 3, I was getting ready for my interview. When I left, I felt calm and confident because I knew exactly where I was going. I got there, answered their questions, and felt really good, except for one thing. The boss seemed indifferent and out of touch in the beginning. I felt it a lot during the interview, but I noticed she slowly came around toward the end of the interview. I thought, *That was very odd.* I wasn't sure about her spirit. I remained open and hopeful because I was sure about myself.

JacQui came to visit me that Thursday, a few days after my interview. We stayed at a hotel so we could have girl talk and catch up on old times. She was excited that I was closer to her part of the world since she and her husband lived in Northern California. But more importantly, she was happy that her time would no longer conflict with her family and me when she'd visit the East Coast. I understood.

I always said to her, "If you're ever on the East Coast and can only find time to call, then do that. I'll be fine. We can always get together at another time."

Yet we always found the time for a quick visit anyway.

On Friday, October 7, we were together, just having lunch on the balcony of the hotel, and my cell phone rang. I answered, hung up, looked at her, and said, "I got the job!"

I interviewed on Monday and got the job on Friday. We celebrated by acting like two kids. We did everything but jump up and down on the beds! We had a good ol' time for the rest of her stay. When we planned her visit in September, we had no idea I'd have an interview that week and then would receive great news while she was in town. Oh my goodness, things had been looking up ever since my first intuitive reading in August and my spiritual healing visit to Sedona in September.

My first day at work was on October 24. I felt something special happening in my life. It's called manifesting. Good things were unfolding in my life at such an alarming pace.

Bring it on! I thought because I was ready, willing, and able to take whatever unfolded. The shift I experienced when I was hospitalized with pneumonia catapulted me in a direction of positive power and energy like never before.

It was my first week at work, and I felt something weird

deep in my spirit. It was an icy cold feeling on the entire floor, full of negativity. I'd managed to find that great high-rise apartment I discovered before leaving the East Coast. Who knew I'd find a job in walking distance from there? I'd be able to walk to work every day. Hallelujah!

I was approved for a unit on the twentieth floor. I really loved the place and the view. But what I loved most was feeling safe. You know, security is important when you live alone. My life had really changed in just a few months.

Meanwhile, my niece helped me to find another car. I had my old 2000 car transported to Arizona. I really loved that thing. It was brand new when I bought it, and I loved not having a car note. I called her Betsy. Betsy never gave me a single day's trouble. She ran great because I never missed a service. I felt bad that Halloween night when I sold her to a company. I even took pictures. It felt odd, strange somewhat, to let her go, but that was consistent with where my life was going. I had to give up all of my past.

When I took my final look at the car, I remembered Barron and my old relationship with him. I had my car for just two days when I met him. Now neither were part of my life. Both treated me great. Betsy made it to Arizona, and she represented a little piece of home, the familiar, my old life. But that was then. I had no complaints. My, how things had changed.

The next day, on November 1, it was time to pick up my newer car. My niece and her husband searched and searched until they found the right one for me. I'm so thankful to them for looking out for me. It's not brand new, but new to me, and I loved it! It took a while to get over my sadness for Betsy. It felt like I had deserted a close friend or family member. I soon got over that and began to appreciate every aspect of my new life. Now I love my car!

That November, I moved into the high-rise apartment on the fifteenth and settled in nicely. My niece helped me pick out all the furniture and odds and ends too. She has a great eye for beauty and fashion. She has excellent taste. She blessed the apartment by burning white sage. She did a great job, and I was comfortable. It felt great!

As I stared out the window of my high-rise apartment, I thought back on how I found a job in September, started the new job, and got rid of my old car in October. I was blessed with another car in my own place by November. I thought about the months that had passed since moving to Arizona because I thought it was amazing how things really do unfold when you're on the right path. I was blown away by so many great things happening just for me.

This may not seem that important to you, but for me, giving up everything helped me to accept change. I came to Arizona knowing that there was much more waiting for me. Personal things can be a crutch or a constant link to the past. My old car was that link to the past for me. I felt at home in that old car while becoming accustomed to Arizona. That old car was the last thing I held on to from my old life back east. It used to feel so good just sitting there in the old girl, which represented so much of my life. It was finally gone now, and I didn't look back.

And that day came when I could finally inhale all the beauty in my new life and exhale the fear, uncertainty, and doubt. I never once focused on what wasn't happening because there was so much going on in my favor. It was hard to believe that life was treating me so well. It felt like I was watching the life of someone else from a distance. Yes, I could actually separate myself and look out into the physical world and see what was happening. My life changed for the best. I was drawn to Arizona for a life-changing experience. Although I still didn't know what that was exactly, I was willing to be patient and wait for the manifestation. I crawled around like a caterpillar for so long, working hard for everything I had back east. Here, everything unfolds with ease. I no longer feel the need or the desire to work hard. Those days are over. I now know that I can manifest through the law of attraction, because thoughts are things. I still need to put action into my desires, but nothing too convoluted. Less really is more.

Finally in Arizona my body stopped functioning in optimum condition. Spirit sent me straight to the hospital with pneumonia in a safe environment for counsel and discussion with my deceased parents about my life. They helped me realize that I have so much work to do, and they sent me back to finish my spiritual journey, my mission.

In reflection, something told me to scout out the place of my employment before the interview. Yes, I know it's common for people to scope out a location in advance of an important meeting. I can't say for sure why I was compelled to go inside the building, take the elevator, and walk down the hall where the interview would take place. I knew before the interview that the job was mine.

Now, with all I had accomplished from June to November, I felt very proud of myself. More importantly, I knew that God carried me in the palm of His hand, as He lifted me into a new reality. I was grateful as I began the next phase of my life, manifesting, believing and trusting while accepting this journey. As my development continues, I remain in hibernation while finding my spirit. Until then, I'd rest in peaceful solitude as I rise into all that I could be while living in my cocoon.

Chapter 7

Awakening

A Renaissance!

I could say that this journey had certainly surprised me in more ways than one. On one hand, I felt more alive than ever, but on the other hand, I had many questions, both contemplated and not. Sometimes I felt like my soul was searching for something and it wouldn't be satisfied until I knew I was following my life's path. After dealing with those feelings for a while, I decided to do something about it. I made my second appointment with Terri for another reading.

But before my appointment, I thought I was haunted. Ugh! A white man kept appearing to me. And since I was clairvoyant, he would also appear both in my mind and visually. At the time, I didn't even know a white man, much less a white man to contact me for any reason. He just stood there and said nothing. I thought *he's very creepy*. I would see him when my eyes were closed or opened. I even saw him at work. I was scared. I was desperate for an answer and for a solution to get this to stop. I literally couldn't wait for my second appointment with Terri, so I called her. She was driving on the 51, but she knew I was afraid.

I said, "Terri, I'm sorry to bother you, but I need your help!"

She asked, "What's going on?"

"There is a man, a white man, who seems to appear everywhere I go, and he's scaring me. I don't know any white men, and I don't know how to make him go away!" I rattled on and on.

She finally stopped me and said, "Don't worry, Jack. He's not trying to scare you. He sees your light, and he's just trying to make a connection with his family."

I felt instant relief and said "Oh, really?"

She said, "Yes. You can control this because you are in control of your life and this situation. All you need to do is say, 'Only close family may appear to me for help because I'm new to this. When I learn more, I'll be able to assist more of you, but until then, just family.'"

I did what she said, and he disappeared, never to return again.

She told me, "You're like a taxicab riding around in the spirit world with your light on! Everyone there who's trying to make a connection sees your light, and they're coming to you for help. They only want to get a message to their family or friends."

I thought, *Oh boy, this is getting serious now.* I'd been scared shitless before, and now I had a freaking light on like a taxicab in the spirit world drawing attention to *me*. What the?!!

When I shared that story with my sisters, my elder sister in particular laughed so hard until she cried. I didn't see that much humor in the story myself, but she certainly did. For a short while, she'd laugh out loud whenever she'd imagine *me* in the spirit world, like a taxicab with *my* light on, attracting spirits.

On December 4, the day for my second appointment for my reading, Terri was really great and prepared with comments for me before I arrived. She answered many questions, and she had inquiries for me as well. After the session, she suggested I develop my clairs in her intuitive studies class coming up next month.

I was surprised on both accounts: because she recommended the class and because she knew I was claircognizant (clear knowing), clairvoyant (clear seeing), and clairaudient (clear hearing), for starters. She said her class began in January and ended in May. I thought about it and thought about it.

I did what I normally do with a new situation. I waited a couple days to let it sink in. But for this, I needed a bit more time. I asked myself, *What in the hell are you about to get yourself into?*

I thought about my childhood and the unusual things that happened. I also pondered about the old elderly friend of the family who used to love to hear me sing and would say to me, "You are a very special child." He was in his late seventies or early eighties back then, and I was seven or eight years old.

I thought about the eerie feelings from years past and how unsettling things were at times. The more I thought about taking the class, the more curious I became. More and more, it started to feel like the right thing to do. So I decided to do it. Just the mere thought of taking the class gave me instant peace. I felt great knowing I had a plan to start the new year.

Lately I was totally uncomfortable at home. I'd think every day, *Something strange is happening. Something very strange.* I was afraid to go to the bathroom at night to tinkle because I felt something in my walk-in closet. The closet was through my bathroom, and I knew something, or someone, was there all the time. I was really scared.

I told my niece about it, and she came over to burn sage again. It felt better for a bit, but in just a few hours, I was back to being afraid. It was so bad until I just resolved to deal with whatever *it* was or find another place to live. I loved my apartment and really did not want to move. I just wanted my fear to go away for good.

One day at home, I connected with my deceased brother who was very determined to speak with his wife and his two daughters. I didn't know what I was doing, but the feeling was so powerful that I allowed him to channel through me. I called my sister-in-law, and they spoke. He was speaking through me, and the conversation was great. I called my niece, his daughter, who lives in the South. Both of his daughters were there, and he used me again to speak to them.

When all of that was done, my body felt extremely tired and very heavy. It's like when you first step out of a pool or the ocean and you can really feel the weight of your body. Well, that feeling stayed with me for a while, and all I could do was rest. I called Terri and asked her about it.

She confirmed and said, "Yes, your brother did indeed channel through you. You are tired because you aren't prepared for that. Class will be a big help in handling those type of situations in the future." I felt validated knowing what I believed, the channeling, really did happen.

"Happy New Year!" I said to myself. It was January 2017, and I was very happy bringing in the new year alone. I flipped channels back and forth, watching the New Year's Eve celebrations. I miss Dick Clark because I saw him every year for decades. But for a short while, I really enjoyed watching Pitbull in Miami. He's such a sexy guy! I think he's an amazing entertainer with great stage presence and a fantastic voice. When all the excitement was over and after speaking with my son and several others in celebration of the new year, I sat, still sipping champagne, and thought about all my accomplishments since moving to Arizona. That's a moment I'll never forget, because it was like I could see my life flash before my eyes. I soon realized that things had worked out great since I uprooted myself from the East Coast just six months earlier.

About a month after I moved into my apartment, I'd feel a little something there. I didn't quite know what it was, but I felt it. Then every once in a while, I'd smell something putrid beneath my kitchen sink. I'd wonder, *How on earth can something smell so bad one day and be completely gone in a few hours or by the next day?*

To top that, I knew there were spirits, a whole lot of them, in my apartment. Each morning, I could feel them there all around me as I dressed. I could feel them in the elevator, as if they'd pack in and ride down with me. Then they'd follow me as I walked to work.

One day, I decided to stop and turn around to see what I was feeling. I can't explain it, but I knew that there were two hundred spirits or more following me and my taxicab light.

I was more than happy to start my new weekly intuitive studies class, which would continue through May. I loved going each Tuesday because that class literally fed my spirit. I was learning about myself and understanding my spiritual gifts.

The first night of class, Terri said, "This is your tribe. Each and every one of you came together tonight not by chance, but by design. All of you planned to meet together right here tonight and to awaken to a certain point together. So take a good look around. You have more in common with each other than you'll ever know."

What a fascinating thing to hear and for her to say. So from January through May, I learned a whole lot about myself, my natural gifts, and my tribe.

Yes, my awakening felt a bit scary at times because I didn't know what was happening in my apartment. After taking a few sessions, I decided to ask about it the next time I went to my intuitive studies class. Terri told me to sage my apartment again. I did. I had a fat bundle of white sage about twelve inches long. I lit that sucker and walked around every nook and cranny I could find. My apartment was smoky, and if anyone had come over, he or she would swear I'd been smoking marijuana.

Having the place blasted with white sage worked for a short while, but spirits would always come right back, like in a day or two. I thought, *What the heck is going on?* I always came to class early to be sure to get a good parking space and my favorite seat. A couple of my tribe members arrived early too, and one day, they waved me over to their car.

One asked, "Are you still feeling all those spirits in your apartment?"

I said, "Hell yeah! They ride with me in my car too!"

She said, "I think you have an open portal at home. That's why you feel so many spirits. It's not your imagination." She told me the information she needed from me in order to confirm if there were a portal or not.

I thanked her and felt better for about one minute. I could hardly concentrate in class because I kept thinking about the fact that I could have an open portal at home. Deep down, I knew it was true because that would explain everything. So I'm sitting in class feeling some kind of way. I could feel my eyes stretch big for a brief moment because my imagination was running wild. I was so scared. It was really tough focusing on the lesson.

Then I had to go home after an intuitive studies class where some of my tribe spoke about their experiences with phenomena that night. This was getting to be too much for me, but I hung in there. I drove home feeling all of those spirits in my car, and I went on up to my unit on the twentieth floor. I played music and slept with the television on. I did that for a couple days until I received word about the portal.

I finally got the call, and she said, "Yes, you definitely have an open portal, and I've closed it forever!"

I said, "What!?"

I was happy, scared, relieved, and overwhelmed all at the same time. I thought about all those spirits sharing space with me. It gave me the creeps! I walked home for lunch the next day to check out the atmosphere. It felt still and very calm, something I hadn't felt for a long time.

When I came home from work at the end of my day, it still felt peaceful. I was so happy that it was finally just me at home. No more unwanted spirits! Now I could get a good night's sleep. I woke up the next day feeling rested for a change.

I find it ironic that, when one door closes, another opens. Now I felt some kind of way at work. I'd been on my new job since October 2016, and I was beginning to feel completely out of place there. I wondered why people seemed to stick to themselves or just in cliques. It was like everyone was on his or her own little private island.

I worked directly with two people, plus my boss and one other person in charge. No one talked. If I said good morning, I felt like I was interrupting their day. If I said good night, I'd interrupted their early evening. This was a very uncomfortable and toxic environment.

Deep in my heart, I knew my pleasantries were not welcomed. So I stopped. I truly understood that people at work didn't have to like me. I got that. But at a young age I was taught to watch my manners and to always treat others as I expected to be treated. I focused on my job and became consumed with my work life because I was never trained for my position and was never given any information to help with my learning curve for this new job.

All this time, I had been learning through trial and error and by asking questions. I was beginning to really dislike where I was. I was feeling the complete opposite of what I felt when my best friend and I celebrated like two kids when I landed that same job.

To make a long story short about working there, things never got better. Everyone remained detached and aloof. Once I understood that, even though it wasn't comfortable, I followed suit and thought, *When in Rome, do as the Romans do.*

I felt sad when my intuitive studies class ended that May. It was like any graduation when you know you may never see many of your friends again. The moments together were remarkable. It was amazing watching everyone grow stronger too. But if we should all come together again, I do understand that it was part of our plan before our incarnation to this planet.

I miss all of my tribe members. But I have to keep moving forward to get closer and closer to my mission. Class was really great. I learned a lot about myself, and I'll always remember those days with love and light.

In August 2017, I had just left the business office in my apartment building. I gave them written notice that I would not renew my lease in November. I had no idea where I'd move to, but I knew things would fall into place, just as they always did back east and since moving to Arizona. The difference is, things were moving much faster here. I would always have fond memories of living in that apartment. During my stay in that apartment, and at work I believe I had learned my lesson, to accept everyone for who and what he or she is. I was never to try to change people because everyone here is on a mission. I also needed to learn to have more compassion in general.

I learned something about myself while living downtown. I didn't like living so close to the homeless. I know that sounds terrible and rather heartless, but it's true. It's not that I thought I was all that, but they were just so dirty. To me, they weren't all there mentally either, and sometimes you'd look around and see them too close or in your space. And since I'm viewed as a clean freak, I thought that seeing the homeless every single day throughout the day was just way too much for me. Turns out that was one of my most valued lessons.

One sunny, pleasant day while walking to see a play at a nearby theatre, I saw a homeless man walk out from a parking lot to the sidewalk. He pulled down his pants, underwear and all. Then he used a brown paper towel to wipe his butt. He raised one leg in the air, wiped himself, and then threw that used funky tissue on the ground. He walked away, pulling up his pants.

I looked up at the sky and asked, "What is my lesson for seeing that?"

As time went by, my heart began to soften toward the homeless. I was changing. Instead of drawing negative power and energy with the homeless, my softened heart drew a more positive reaction out of me. I began to see them as regular people out in the world, doing the best they could. They were on level two of Maslow's hierarchy of needs, but they didn't have the finances to support themselves. They no longer bothered me, not even when they'd ask for money.

Throughout my life, I've always given the homeless money, but that was only because I'd see them in passing or would see someone with a sign at a red light. I didn't see them each and every day throughout the day as I do now. That's why this situation was so different. When I realized what was happening to me, it took a while, but I came around, like *How the Grinc Stole Christmas.*

I had a new capacity for love, like the Grinch in the end, and nonjudgment like never before. Yes, I started giving again, but not every day. I realized that where I worked was involved and played a big role in the homeless crisis by helping with the homelessness problem for years.

A homeless man walked up to me and asked if he could get a burger at 5 Guys. He said, "I don't want money. I just need you to go inside with me and pay for a sandwich."

I said, "Okay."

We went inside, and I was prepared to buy a sandwich. I said to him, "Go on and place the order."

He said, "Yeah, I want a cheeseburger, a large order of fries, and a large Coke."

I looked at him, smiled, and thought, *So much for just a burger.* I chuckled inside and helped him figure out everything he wanted on his cheeseburger. I paid for his meal, he thanked me, and I walked home. I think that particular moment was a test that I passed.

I understand that paying for a meal or two doesn't count

for much, but what it does is show that I hold no distain when I see the homeless. I see people, men, women, and children doing the best they can, day by day. We all need food, shelter, and clothing. We all need a good night's rest. We all need to feel acknowledged and not judged. And yes, we all need a little help from time to time.

Help could mean a friendly chat on the phone or a surprise visit from a dear friend. Help is not always monetary. It's sometimes great to give time and attention to another human being. Yes, I put myself out there and exposed a character flaw within myself. I'm not proud of how I once felt, but I am proud about how far I've come. I spotted that apartment building while still living on the East Coast. I moved there and learned to never, ever judge anyone because I don't know his or her story. We all have a story. Some of us are better at hiding our truths than others are. So now, when I see homeless individuals, couples, or families, I don't judge. But rather I wonder, *What is your story?* Yes, I'm ashamed by my initial feelings toward the homeless. It's a lesson well learned.

I was becoming too consumed by my work environment. I retired from my job back east because of the toxic environment. I felt sick to my stomach and just unwell all over back then. I lost patches of hair on the top of my head, and a patch fell out midway, on down to the back of my head.

I saw my doctor, and she said, "It's past time for you to make a change at work."

That time, I was finally prepared to give her an answer. I said, "I'm retiring in June and relocating to Arizona."

She was very happy for me and said that the warm weather would be great for my bones. It turned out that my hair loss was due to stress. That was back in 2015 at my old job.

I brought up that old situation because it mirrors exactly what my body was feeling today. I was starting to have those same feelings creep up once again. My health had started to domino in the wrong direction with one thing leading to another.

So I discussed resigning with my niece and my oldest sister. They both agreed that I should resign without hesitation. They were concerned about my health, but not more worried than I was. I found peace in knowing I'd be leaving soon.

A coworker resigned and moved to another state late August. She wasn't that helpful. My second coworker was still there being herself. Labor Day holiday was great! I needed that break from work. I knew it was time for me to get out of my work situation.

On September 18, I submitted my letter of resignation, about a month before my one-year anniversary there. That following week, I found out that my second coworker was leaving her position in a few days. She never told me herself that she was leaving. Nonetheless, I felt a great sense of relief when I decided to resign. Not only did I resign from there, I decided to walk away from working on a nine-to-five job for good. It felt good knowing I'd be leaving this toxic environment.

And that day came when I soon realized that a regular nine-to-five was not good for my health. This time, it would not take eighteen years to actually do something about it, but rather just ten months to know that it wasn't working out and I was to trust that everything would work out like it always did.

My physical well-being is very important to me. Without that, I wouldn't be able to fulfill my spiritual mission and help others as well. I'm getting closer to my spiritual assignment, but I'm still searching for answers.

In reflection, the fear I experienced in my apartment was a different kind because it was related to the spirit world. I know now that I wasn't haunted, but rather visited by many spirits who simply wanted my help to connect with their loved ones. I wasn't ready to assist them. I couldn't ask if the types of spirts that came through the portal when it was open were good or not so good. I don't want to know that answer, not while I'm still living here.

Later I found out that spirits of all kinds enter through portals or gateways. I was able to stay and enjoy my apartment because of a better understanding of my environment, both inside and out. Things never seem as bad or scary when you have answers. I had a mixture of two worlds there, which caused uncertainty and doubt. But now I relished in the realization of getting closer to my mission. I had to learn the hard lesson of nonjudgment. Oh, what an awakening!

Chapter 8

Rising

Always Trust

Oh my goodness! This job was crazy. I was enlightened to the fact that my coworker who moved to another state was groomed for my position. The pieces of that puzzle were sliding right into place. I also found out that my two coworkers didn't really like each other. I honestly thought they did. I used to hear them from my office chatting away, and I'd wonder why they never found anything to say to me. Oh well. Now I realized that, every time I asked the one who moved for help, she was very pleasant, but I was sure she might have been pissed off every time I called her name or went to her with a question. I sensed it every time, but just couldn't put my finger on it. But somehow I knew I was the last person she wanted to ask her anything.

I took both of them to lunch for the Christmas holiday. We arrived at the restaurant, and no one said a word. I thought to myself, *What kind of shit is this?!*

137

It was so bad until I said, "Hey, guys, nobody's talking. Why's everyone so quiet?"

They managed to squeeze something out only because I said something. This was the absolute worst lunch I have ever had in my entire life. We left, they thanked me, and we all went back to work like nothing ever happened. I couldn't help but feel like I had wasted my time, energy, money, and effort in trying to bring us together to establish a better work rapport because everything stayed the same. Now I know why. Pure hatred and abomination filled the air in my work environment. This is why I call it toxic.

As I mentioned, one resigned and relocated. To make matters worse for me, it was assumed that I would take on all her duties on top of my own responsibilities. Now I know all about hard work and burning the late-night oil straight into the next day. Extra work never bothered me, but what did irk me was the total disregard and lack of respect for my role and me. My boss or the number two in charge never took the time to discuss the transition when my coworker resigned and the impact her resignation would have on the office and me. I deserved that conversation, but it never happened.

What's hurtful is that I know, through my claircognizance, that the thought of holding a meeting with me regarding the transition never, ever occurred to either one of them. It simply never entered their minds. I knew deep in my heart that nothing was done in malice, but executed nonetheless.

The entire office malfunctioned due to the lack of communication, separatism, and cliques. I, therefore, decided to work in self-imposed exile. The less I saw anyone, the better. I am a sensitive person and clairsentient too. I was simply tired of coming home completely drained every day because I allowed myself to pass by those ill-willed spirits who meant me no good. My spirit literally battled with their spirits every day, which was draining. At the end of the day, I felt better when I took the long way around to and from my office where I passed no one.

Work was piling in left and right. It was on a Friday when someone came to my office with mail in her hands and asked, "Who's checking the mail?" She had much attitude in her voice too.

I looked up. "I don't know. I do check the mail when I'm in that area, but it might not be every day."

She glared at me. "Well, mail comes every day."

I wanted to rush over and tackle her like Dave Butz. Yes, I'm a die-hard Washington Redskins football fan and have been for nearly forty years. I don't recall what I said next, but it took everything in me to physically control myself. I remember briefly looking down to see if blood dripped from my mouth from biting my tongue so hard to remain professional and spiritual, a truly ebb-and-flow moment. She just didn't know whom she had approached.

Luckily for her, I caught myself and realized that I was on a higher frequency from years before. Oh, it would have been so on, without a doubt. She would have never, ever approached me or anyone else with something so trivial and stupid like that again.

She was not going to cause me to spiritually come down to her level. Although I did come very close to doing just that, I suddenly realized that event was the last straw. I had enough. I would no longer tolerate feeling like Cinderella sitting "In My Own Little Corner."

Back to work that following Monday, I received a very special message from an earth angel who paved the way for me. The angel said, "The matter has always been in your hands. You control the outcome. Don't wait. Submit your letter of resignation today."

I listened and did just that. I felt instant relief and back on track with my spiritual awakening.

When you're on your spiritual path, things really do work out. I've learned to trust that spirit will not lead me astray. My job was just fine at first. I was sent there as part of my transition to Arizona, my mission, and as part of my awakening. It was a test. I can see that it took me too long to finally say "When!" Esther Hicks talks about the ocean's cycle of ebb and flow, and this was one of those moments. I'm not upset with myself for carrying my cross up a steep hill at work. It taught me that my will is stronger than that entire office and my purpose is to stay with my positive higher vibration for continued power and energy.

I love myself unconditionally, and I love others as well. I mistakenly thought that most people followed the golden rule: Do unto others as you would have them do unto you. That's what I live by. I also know that some people never consider those words. That's all right too. I was meant to feel the tension and the disrespect, and I was meant to feel demeaned so I'd never feel comfortable. And that was what got me moving.

With the strength and protection of Archangel Michael,

I would continue following the golden rule as I spent these last days on this job. Two days after submitting my letter of resignation, I found out that my other coworker would leave in a week. I'd be the only one there to assist bosses one and two. "Well, I'll be damned!"

The more you know, the more you'll grow. After the intuitive studies class, I decided to study mediumship through the Morris Pratt Institute. I started the home study course in July 2017 and finished that following September. Today, I am a proud Morris Pratt graduate. When I look back to the year before, July 2016, I developed pneumonia and visited with my parents in the spirit world. Today, I have the skills of a developing medium, which means I have the ability to properly communicate with spirit, or I know how to tap into the other side, the spirit world.

I haven't assisted or invited unrelated spirits yet because I'm still growing in all respects and continuing to learn while loving every minute of it. I still have flashbacks of when I was petrified, living in my own space because of my taxicab light!

There is so much behind the law of attraction. I'd unwittingly been practicing that law ever since I decided to give up everything on the East Coast and begin my new life in Arizona. Things had progressed for me at a very fast pace because I put it out there with clear expectation and intention. I really learned to manifest.

I was now focused on meditation. I came here with my eyes wide open while seeing myself already enjoying my new life. I expected nothing less. I was not surprised when I got the job at that company. I was destined to be there. I knew I'd live in the high-rise apartment in walking distance to that very same place of work. I came to Arizona with intentions in place, and the power and energy took a dip for a bit and picked up once again. So far, all of my expectations had been met. Yes, I had learned to manifest and recognize when it happens.

I guess you can tell that I was truly affected by the lessons learned at my last nine-to-five job. I just want people to act like people and not like robots. Why is it so hard for people to discuss business matters face-to-face? Why do we feel the need to send emails or text messages when we sit just a few steps away from each other? Whatever happened to common courtesy? Is it so wrong to care about your work family? Yes, I said work family because we spend so many hours together beneath the same roof.

Is the workplace like a mirror of today's American family— full of detachment, resentment, aloofness, dishonesty, and the lack of face-to-face communication? Have electronics and gadgets taken away human nature and human kindness? Does it take a workplace tragedy to bring folks closer together?

I feel strongly about each question because our approach to life in general affects us all. In this instance, less is not more. We are all human beings incarnated in this physical body on earth to complete a mission. Since we all know that love is the most powerful tool we have to complete any mission, spiritual or not, then why aren't we using it?

And that day came when I realized I let myself down once again by accepting yet another boring office job when I relocated. That was my time to shine and do something that I really enjoyed, like finding a nice job in the arts. But this time, I wouldn't beat up on myself and feel bad about accepting what felt normal or comfortable at the time. It took no time at all for me to realize that working there was like working with robots in human appearance. I could move on with a clear conscience, knowing I did all I could do to make a difference in that workplace.

What was very clear to me is that I was shown that my spirit and work ethics were tested, and I knew that I would be missed when I left. That's not patting myself on the back. Instead it's realized development in my claircognizance (clear-knowing) or clairsentience (clear-sensing) or through realized development in my clairvoyance (extrasensory perception [ESP]), or sixth sense. Or simply put in this regard, it's just an observation.

In reflection, I got that job at the perfect time. It's quite clear that God had a plan for me. He provided a safe place for me to land on my feet after arriving in Arizona. Soon after, He made me take a good look in the mirror to stop judging the homeless and others. That job paid the bills, which led to my self-confidence while experiencing fear, uncertainty, and doubt at home. That job was a place where some people showed true character and involvement in the homeless issues, where I was once severely lacking. That job was there for me, keeping me going as I developed my clairs. Working there and taking my intuitive studies class was a very hard lesson learned in ebb and flow, yin and yang. That is, I was doing what I liked and disliked at the same time, which allowed me to really see the light and take heed to the messages from an angel who advised me to make a move. As Abraham would say, "When you know what you don't like helps you to know what you do like."

I awakened more and more each day that passes, which brought me closer to my mission. While interacting with all people with nonjudgment, I would freely move on with an evolving spiritual purpose. And I would freely move on, trusting my inner spirit and higher self that is bright and rising.

Chapter 9

The Divine

Love Thyself

Who is the Divine? We all know that there is more to all of this domain that we inhabit. I know now that I am spirit first, occupying a human body, and here on a mission. To complete the mission I signed up for before coming here, I made an agreement, which is my mission.

After entering this realm through birth, I came to be. *Hello, I'm here!* Part of my earthly plan before my arrival was also choosing my parents. I chose them out of all the people living on this planet because the two of them together would provide that special something that I needed to complete my mission. It's been challenging to realize my plan and activate my mission, because it's designed for me to forget the minute I take my first breath here on Earth. Part of my mission is to wake up and remember. It's strange that I knew my entire plan when I in my mother's womb. But every day since birth, I remember nothing. That's called "being asleep." Yes, being asleep is also part of the plan because we must factor in the human experience before we wake up.

When we come to earth, we know that we'll lose that information, that very powerful information that holds the blueprint for who we really are and what we are here to do. We also know that we'll forget the boundless gifts we possessed on the day of our arrival until we begin to wake up and realize who we are and why we're here. We are all special beings on Planet Earth. We are all waking up at different moments in time, and we hone our intuitive skills at our own pace. We grow as we learn and accept our intuitive abilities each day.

Obviously our development is not a race. It just is. I've accepted my wake-up call from the Divine as planned. My earthly free will has finally helped me to align with my mission, to spread consciousness by helping others to wake up. And now it's my duty to awaken more and more each day so I may continue on with my mission, just as my deceased parents pointed out to me when we met for that nanosecond. According to my plan of action with all my guardian angels who dwell in the spirit world on a higher vibration in golden-white light, I will not rest until I've done what I came here to do.

Whether it's God, the Divine, Great Spirit, Source, or no matter what name is used to call upon this infinite intelligence, I choose to call him God or Source, the one who sends His love and light to all of us, as we are communicating and vibrating with the same divine spirit. My earthly free will inspires me to say "Him" because, as in earthly English grammar, I choose to reference Source as "He," as it is used when the gender is unknown.

Yes, I realize that there is much debate about using sexist terms. But this is not about a sex or man or woman. It's simply about how I choose to use my earthly free will as it relates to earthly speech, while fully realizing that infinite intelligence is neither he nor she. But for the sake of this chapter, I simply wanted to explain how I came up with the term "He" as I reference Source henceforth.

When you're in alignment with your life's purpose, everything unfolds in divine order and with perfectly timed power and energy in the direction of whatever success you've imagined and attracted. Success can be setting a date to clean your closet. You will feel great to finally walk in or see your organized closet. Something as simple as that, ridding clutter, is something to really smile about because your personal space matters. Did you know that the amount of clutter in your home represents the quantity of clutter in your mind?

Studies have shown that physical clutter in your surroundings can have a negative impact on your ability to focus and process information. I wanted to touch on clutter because, if you are thinking about strengthening your intuitive abilities, I would first start by removing clutter in your surroundings at work and home. That would have an immediate positive impact, which brings in the law of attraction and positive power and energy.

In my experience, clutter doesn't mean negative power and energy, but rather it's power and energy at a full stop. That means you have stagnated yourself from growth. You are at a halt, which impacts your spirituality.

Early on in my intuitive studies class, I came to a halt and found it very difficult to connect spiritually. That was because of the clutter at home with an excessive amount of spirits who flowed through from an open portal in my walk-in closet. We had homework each week, giving a classmate a reading by email, and I needed to connect and tap in at home to complete the assignments. I managed to get through that and did a fine job as well, but until my classmate assisted me by closing that portal in my apartment, I would not have found intuitive studies interesting at all. Fortunately I had the insight, or claircognizance, to share the experience of feeling and sensing all those spirits in class with my tribe. Without doing so, I would not have connected to receive the power and energy that brought forth the spiritual help I needed. It gives me pause to think that I may not be as spiritually connected as I am today, without the help of my intuitive studies tribe.

Since class ended May 2017 and with all clutter removed, I was able to complete the Morris Pratt course. It means I have reached such a level in my development that I am now able to help more people and pets by tapping in and giving spiritually inspired messages from the other side. I believe in the continuity of life because I believe in mediumship. A medium provides proof in the continuity of life and the realization of the spirit world. As a developing medium, I too have delivered messages from the spirit world.

The Divine has shown me time and time again that whatever I'm going through that's perceived as negative and questionable is never as bad as it seems after you sleep on it. A certain spiritual recharge happens only through sleep, which includes naps. Have you noticed that in your own life?

No matter what the problem may be, when you go to bed, sleep, and wake up the next day, the problem is still there, but that overwhelming contrary feeling is gone. Now the feeling is no longer overwhelming, and you're actually able to think it through and make a sound decision. That's because clutter has been removed from the unwanted situation and your ability to make a sound decision or give advice has been restored.

Remember, we are creators who make our own reality. Thoughts really are things. I was consumed with pleasant thoughts when I started my new job. I was very hopeful that I would fit in and would be liked and respected as a professional and a person. With all my effort, which was part of my spiritual lesson, I learned that my place in life is not in an office space. I had to learn once and for all that I am best while helping others through spirit readings and messages. I know now that my gifts really are appreciated. My classmates, my tribe, told me so.

Nearing the end of our time together and for the final night of homework, the lady I chose as my homework partner said she was hoping I'd choose her because she heard so many wonderful things about me from others, and she saw me as a person of deep spirituality. I was surprised and very humbled.

My intuitive studies class provided a great spiritual foundation for further growth and development. I will be eternally grateful to Terri for intuitive skills training that helped shape my future. I am working my mission while understanding my natural gifts. Now it's up to me to spread the word and continue growing while moving on to the next phase of my life. I look forward to what life has to offer and to what this incarnation unfolds next. I remain open to all possibilities. I remain at peace, knowing that I'm on the right path, a path to help others to wake up and start their mission.

And that day came when I realized that my entire life isn't what it seems. Nothing I've experienced is real. I know I am a spirit occupying a human body for the purpose of my planned mission here on earth. Soon as we embark on the fifth dimension, we will all see the world from different eyes and bodies. We will know that love is everyone's most powerful weapon as we accept our mission. But how you show, teach, and give it is up to you. It may be too simple for many, but sending and sharing love is the answer. Think about it. Where would we be without love?

In reflection, God never takes us down the wrong road. We tend to sometimes choose the road most travelled, which ultimately has the most obstacles to overcome our learning lessons, but it's not a wrong route. It's the road that many of us insist on travelling because we've been conditioned that nothing good comes easy.

But that's not true. God also provides us with the road less travelled, which is the one with the least amount of problems, obstacles, and resistance. It is the spiritual path that takes a lot of readiness on your part, something most of us are still working on. Otherwise you'll get to your goal, but with much effort. His spiritual road is the road of least resistance and is full of love, peace, and harmony by design. He is there for all of us. He is Source, our Creator, and the Divine.

Chapter 10

The Journey Begins

Love and Light

"I love myself unconditionally." I'm getting closer and closer to making that a reality each day. I think and say that to myself all the time so I have positive power and energy building rather than the opposite. It's taken me many years to thrive in that realization and work at it day by day. I've learned that love is the most powerful gift that each of us has as spirit. It is also the hardest thing to sometimes prove or show. That's the ebb and flow of our incarnation. There is no good or bad, just lessons. It takes every moment in our lives to become who we are and where we are in our lives. We will either continue learning the same lessons through repetition, or we will finally get it when we stop, think about what we are doing, learn from the lesson, and move on.

It took me a while to really get it. I repeated one lesson in love twice. I won't rehash all of those two stories, but my first lesson was an eight-year relationship experience with Andy, a very fascinating older guy. My second lesson on the same topic was my sixteen-year relationship with Barron, a marathon, but after twenty-four combined years of learning one lesson, I finally got it. Again, this shows that there is no right or wrong way to learn a lesson. We have free will to either choose the road full of obstacles or to choose the path of least resistance.

For me, it was proof that I was still obstacle-driven in choosing a mate. But after many years of the same lesson, I am far better off because of it. As Abraham would say, "Knowing what you don't want helps you know what you do want. There are no mistakes."

In this case and after years of learning my lessons in love, I finally know what I want, and I'm attracting a fantastic guy who resonates with me and is aligned with me. He's out there somewhere. Meanwhile, as Abraham would say, I'm getting ready to be ready to be ready for when we meet.

After my relationship with Andy, I declared, "I will never date another older man again. I will never be in another long-term relationship that doesn't lead to marriage."

Well, I've shared with you that, not only was I attracted to yet another older guy, fifteen years older in fact, I managed to remain in that relationship twice as long (sixteen years), and that relationship did not lead to marriage either. How's that for the law of attraction? I got exactly what I said I didn't want. That's how the law of attraction works.

In other words, you will attract the very thing you work so hard to avoid, which means your attention is focused on what you don't want. When we work very diligently and focused on what we don't want, we attract what we don't want because we've given it the power and energy. Instead we should focus on what we do want and give that the power and energy.

I simply could have said after my eight-year relationship with Andy came to a crash, "The next guy will be my age and will be someone who's very nice, confident, and unafraid of commitment." Or something to that effect.

Do you see the difference? I was so focused on what I didn't want and found Barron. If I had changed my focus to what I did want, things would be very different for me today. That was a very long lesson to learn. Thank God that's a thing of the past.

Andy and Barron taught me to believe what a man says out of his mouth right from the beginning and to always put myself first. In hindsight, I do appreciate both relationships very deeply because, without those lessons, I would not be the person I am today. I've learned to treat myself like the queen that I am.

When I finally bought my one-way ticket to Arizona, I treated myself with a first-class ticket. That one small gesture set aside just for me was my way of paying attention to my wants because it's up to me to take care of my needs. I also started treating myself to some of my wants every chance I get.

Yes, I know that has nothing to do with my intuitive connection, but it does have everything to do with my state of mind, which inevitably helps with my connection to spirit. This is a tried-and-true method that works for me. I'm not saying that you should do as I've done. No, quite the opposite. I gave my example, hoping it would ignite something in you too to do something special for yourself your way! Do whatever brings happiness to you, and that happiness will start the power and energy for more happiness and so on. It really does work.

The material things we buy and love so much mean nothing. It's all about what makes you happy and about the love, compassion, and nonjudgment shown toward others. Find the courage to do what it takes to energize and jump-start your mind. When you're able to get rid of clutter in your life, you'll soon feel the love for yourself begin to blossom like a beautiful rose. When you master loving yourself and putting your needs first, you will master the heartfelt art of being kind to others. If it takes something as trivial as treating yourself to a want sometimes to start the power and energy to love thyself, then by all means do it. Start right where you are.

Know that these moments of joy will help your mind to awaken to what really matters. Do what it takes for you to get moving. That's all I'm saying. For some, it may be making a decision to buy or give away a big-ticket item you've always wanted or loved. That experience is a lesson in trust. Of course, it does not mean to do something on a whim. But think about it, and think it through without clutter. You'll be amazed by your own inner strength and clarity about many situations, which leads to better decision making.

It took something a bit more drastic on my part to continue down the road of spiritual awareness. I had to uproot my entire life and move clear across the country to figure that out. It was the best move I ever made in my life. It was my destiny and my spiritual plan to be riffed from my long-term employer. It was also my plan to return to that same employer, dejected, hurt, and feeling unappreciated. Those constant feelings steadied my level of discomfort, discontent, and disregard. My return was never peaceful. I always felt like I was just flapping around like a fish out of water for those two years. I finally retired.

It was my destiny to land a job in Arizona in my comfort zone, doing the same type of work I swore I'd never do again. Unaware at the time, I gave what I didn't want to give, which was my power and energy once again. This time around it took less than a year for me to see the light and know that I didn't belong there. And I resigned soon after.

All these painful lessons were meant to be. Every single one has brought me closer to my full potential intuitively. As a young medium, I remember watching *Medium*. I never missed an episode, and when that show ended, I felt a deep sadness. Before then, I felt that same type of deep sadness when *Touched by an Angel* concluded.

I have always been drawn to shows that involved love, faith, and spirituality. I also love science fiction in TV shows and movies such as *V*, *Fringe*, *Star Trek*, *The Matrix*, *Fifth Element*, and others. Did those shows stir my spirituality and cause me to question my reality? I think so. It was during those days that I began to question my work and myself.

God, Ascended Master Jesus, legion of angels, spirit guides, higher self, parents, grandparents, brother, aunts, uncles, and all my ancestors helped me to have a loving and peaceful awakening. This is an acknowledgement to those who helped me connect to a higher vibration, a higher frequency in the spirit world. This is a message I received from my angels, and I happily pass it on to each of you:

"You are who you think you are. If you simply do the work that leads you to your path where doors are never closed, you'd soon realize that those doors were never there. It was all in your mind. Know that you follow a path fully protected in the divine golden-white light. Go with enlightenment to fulfill your mission."

Those inspired words came to me during my regular morning meditation on June 28, 2017. In numerology, that date equates the angel number eight, which tells you to step into your personal power; to have faith and trust in your own abilities, skills, and talents; and to use those skills and talents to your highest potential. That was definitely another wake-up call for me as I had no idea I'd receive a message from my angels that morning. My angels were encouraging me, as they always do, to keep on going. They wanted me to know that it takes great understanding and trust to walk the path in the golden-white light of the Divine.

And that day came when I knew that I was on my spiritual journey. I know I am still evolving, seeking, and understanding myself and my blueprint each day. This book is a tiny step toward that mission. More importantly, I hope that, by sharing my story, I've helped someone who may be new to understanding his or her intuitive gifts. Through this book, it is my intent to help newly awakened spirits to move on to the next step in finding that higher spiritual vibration and frequency. It is my hope that this book will help you to move forward in your life so you are living at your very best.

In reflection, it took a while for me to trust and believe. I guess my initial reaction was very human. I finally realized that I am here to provide a service to many people, consciousness. It's a service to help others understand their feelings of knowing there's a lot more to life than what meets the eye. My service also includes assisting with more awakenings by arousing and explaining curious thought patterns in my books.

As I mentioned in chapter 7, I too am relatively new to all that comes with awakening. But I welcome the newness with opened arms. I am free to gain all the knowledge I can about myself and the world, both inside myself and out. I accept the fact that I'm on a path with great spiritually inspired power and energy. Knowing what I really want out of life and the journey of manifesting backed by action and receiving on my end heralds all the new experiences that the Divine sends my way. Good luck to all of you as you awaken and realize why you're here. Love and light to you all.

The journey continues.

Afterword

I have taken a leap of faith with God, Source, Infinite Intelligence, Great Creator, and all of my guardian angels who are with me as I spread my wings and fly in an awakened state of mind. I am so honored to be the vessel, a link with a message to help others. I accepted the charge wholeheartedly, which came directly from Source to spread love and light around the world.

He summoned me early one morning during meditation with the brightest pulsating light I've ever seen, coupled with an overwhelming feeling of love. He spoke clearly to me, not in words, and said, "Go and send love and light to all."

I'll never, ever forget that morning or that truly indescribable loving feeling. I didn't want to leave! I wanted to stay right there with Source. But I heard the call and accepted my mission here on earth, and it's taken me on a new direction, a fresh life path.

Now I'm here to help assist all who've recently awakened and those who feel they are in a tangled web of earthly limitation. It is my duty to help lift you above all doors because there are no doors in the spirit world. Everything leads upward to love and light.

This book is the first of a series. It is important to understand that the first step to enlightenment is acceptance. After I investigated, participated, and understood the magnificent shift in my spirit, mind, and body, it took no effort at all to accept all of the newness, joy, and happiness that this shift brought to my life. Although my new life resonates with me, I still need to work on myself and continue to grow stronger in the knowledge of this great shift, one that we are all facing that has ushered us all into the fifth dimension, another story within itself.

Several books out there describe and share with you exactly what the fifth dimension is. So find a book and author that resonates with you. Then buy that book and read it with an open mind for a clear understanding of what is happening on Planet Earth today.

I will continue writing this series with the intention of helping others through angelically inspired words because I realize there must be others who are waking up. My goal is to assist by using my life as an example of how I woke up and let others know that there's nothing to be afraid of. I want everyone who reads this book to feel refreshed, enlightened, and inspired to step into his or her own reality by seeking out those nearby who can take you further along. There is much yet to learn for all of us. I will be sure to share my growth in my next book.

Yes, Archangels Michael, Gabriel, and Raphael have been with me throughout this entire project and will remain throughout the entire series and thereafter. I write because

I love it, and I hope you'll stay with me until I complete the series. It's amazing how I had hints of writing as far back as the early 1980s. *Murder She Wrote* was my absolute favorite show. I loved watching how Jessica Fletcher lived her life. She wrote books and travelled the world. She was a guest lecturer and helped solve cases and more. I was drawn by the fact that she did what she wanted to do on her time. I always wanted to live like that, enjoying life while doing something that I love well into aging. When you do what you love and it also helps others, you can do that something until you transition. For me, that something is writing. I can see myself writing well into my future because it brings me great joy.

I remember many days from my past and relish in my present, which is very surprisingly enlightening. This life is such a blessing, such a gift. That's why I remain focused on what the day brings, which means fully appreciating each day in that light. I've learned to appreciate all of it, and I do mean all of it because that's how we learn and grow. It's up to all of us, light workers, earth angels, and indigo, crystal, and rainbow children, among others, to assist humanity in this new dimension. There is so much to be seen and done. I'm on the side of light, helping with that mission.

I will do everything I can to help others through writing, mediumship, continuing education, volunteering, and spreading love and light. I want the world to be filled with positive light, power, and energy full of love and peace. If we all focused on love every day throughout the day, the world will be a much better place. I'm willing to do all that I can to send love and light to all, including those who appear in opposition. Remember, it takes love to crack the surface of the minds of powerful world leaders who may be filled with negative energy. Sincere thoughts of love can thwart those thoughts. When we counter negative energy, our hearts must be sincere when we do send love and light because God knows our heart.

I hope you've enjoyed my first book. I'm already inspired to begin and complete the next. But before that project begins, the Great Pyramids of Giza in Cairo beckoned me to come home, as well as the great city of Petra, Jordan. I'll spend some time over there in early 2018 at the Great Pyramids and along the Nile River, and I'll see the great sacred land of Petra in Jordan. I'll be sure to share my experiences there as well as my continued growth in spiritual development and enlightenment in my next book. Until then, love thyself and remember to send love and light to all.